What People Are Saying
About *Uncrushed*

"Beth is uniquely gifted at both inviting us into lament and helping us discover joy in the middle of our grief. She not only writes about living *Uncrushed*, she embodies it, and this book will show you how to as well."

—Davey Blackburn, Speaker, Author, Founder
of Nothing is Wasted Ministries

"*Uncrushed* is a warm hug for the grieving heart–a cozy place to cry when you need to cry, and laugh when you need to laugh. Compelling stories of deep love, crushing loss, and how the Lord can turn our mourning into dancing."

—Bob Goff, New York Times bestselling author
of *Love Does; Everybody, Always; Dream Big; Live
in Grace, Walk in Love;* and *Undistracted*

"*Uncrushed* is so much more than a book about coping with the loss of a loved one. It's a guide through grief in all its unwieldy forms. If you've lost someone you love, you're sitting in the wreckage of a miscarriage or marriage that ended, or are grieving the past or 'what could have been,' Beth will be both a welcomed friend and trusted guide through the chaotic emotions and insurmountable mountain that mourning- in all its forms- can be."

—Krista Ortiz, Co-Pastor, Meta Church, NYC

"Let's face it. Most of us aren't good with grief. No one wants to become an expert at it, but if you live long enough, grief always shows up, either in our lives or those we love. It's why Beth's book is such a gift. She shows us we don't have to run from grief. We can find healing, restore our joy and eventually show others how to as well."

—Jeff Henderson, Entrepreneur, speaker, business leader, and President of The FOR Company

"Beth is joy and resilience personified. Her journey through life's valleys and the story of God's goodness at every turn has grown my faith and left me inspired to keep on walking through the valleys I'm led through with abounding joy. Beth's life and this book have impacted me deeply and I know it will impact yours."

—Dan Lian, Teaching Pastor, NewSpring Church

"Beth Marshall is more than a terrific writer. She's a true friend and trusted voice when it comes to the area of grieving and loss. We've known Beth for nearly two decades and we've seen her not only navigate her own pain, but help others tread through the darkness to find hope and light on the other side. We cannot wait for you to read *Uncrushed.* Trust us–read it slowly because you do not want to miss a single word."

—Clayton and Sharie King, NewSpring Church and Crossroads Ministries

"*Uncrushed* is exactly what people experiencing grief need. Author Beth Marshall provides space for the raw emotions and questions that flood in, while gently guiding us through courageous steps of healing. Through her humble, helpful, and even hilarious words, we know we are not alone, opening up hope that we can live *Uncrushed.*"

—Jessye Wilden, bestselling author of *We Wrote Your Name in Color: A Memoir*

"Powerful lessons on surviving grief delivered with humor, wisdom, faith and a cast of remarkable characters who "graduated to heaven too soon." Thank you, Beth Marshall, for teaching us how to restore joy after the loss of a loved one and for honoring the memory of those we've lost. (Aunt) Beazy's love shines through your pages."

—David Montgomery, Attorney

"Beth Marshall is the friend we all need to help us navigate the murky waters of grief. If you've felt stuck in your grief journey or haven't known how to help loved ones walking through loss, *Uncrushed* is the perfect guidebook. I'm so grateful to have this resource to share with friends during their times of loss. Thank you, Beth, for helping us live joyfully in the legacies of the loved ones we've lost."

—Erin Frist, Engage Real Estate Group

Uncrushed

real steps for
healing your grief
and restoring your joy

BETH MARSHALL

END GAME
Press

Uncrushed

Copyright © 2023 by Beth Marshall
All rights reserved.

No part of this work may be reproduced or transmitted in any form or by any means, electronic or mechanical, including photocopying and recording, or by any information storage or retrieval system, except as may be expressly permitted by the 1976 Copyright Act or in writing from the publisher. Requests for permission can be emailed to info@ endgamepress.com.

End Game Press books may be purchased in bulk at special discounts for sales promotion, corporate gifts, ministry, fund-raising, or educational purposes. Special editions can also be created to specifications. For details, contact Special Sales Dept., End Game Press, P.O. Box 206, Nesbit, MS 38651 or info@endgamepress.com.

Visit our website at www.endgamepress.com.

Library of Congress Control Number: 2022952475

Hardback ISBN: 978-1-63797-080-5
Paperback ISBN: 978-1-63797-108-6
eBook ISBN: 978-1-63797-091-1

Cover Design by Bruce Gore
Interior Design by Typewriter Creative Co.

Scriptures marked NIV are taken from The New International Version (NIV): Scripture Taken From The Holy Bible, New International Version ®. Copyright© 1973, 1978, 1984, 2011 By Biblica, Inc.™. Used by permission of Zondervan. All rights reserved worldwide. www.zondervan.com The "NIV" and "New International Version" are trademarks registered in the United States Patent and Trademark Office by Biblica, Inc.™

"Scripture quotations marked (ESV) are from The ESV® Bible (The Holy Bible, English Standard Version®), copyright © 2001 by Crossway, a publishing ministry of Good News Publishers. Used by permission. All rights reserved."

Scripture quotations are taken from the Holy Bible, New Living Translation, copyright ©1996, 2004, 2015 by Tyndale House Foundation. Used by permission of Tyndale House Publishers, Carol Stream, Illinois 60188. All rights reserved.

Scripture quotations marked MSG are taken from THE MESSAGE, copyright © 1993, 2002, 2018 by Eugene H. Peterson. Used by permission of NavPress, represented by Tyndale House Publishers. All rights reserved.

Printed in India
10 9 8 7 6 5 4 3 2 1

Table of Contents

Section Nine: Staying Uncrushed

Bonus Chapters

Introduction

H ave you ever gotten news that literally took your breath away? I surely have. It was the late-night call that my mom—my healthy, hilarious, newlywed mom—was gone. Nobody could have imagined her happily-ever-after ending so quickly. As weeks marched by, the shock wore off and I was left wondering—*What do you do with all this pain?*

After months of trying to outrun the ache—and sprint toward some imaginary silver lining—I realized that running from the pain leaves you crushed, lonely, and confused. In that desperate season, the Lord gently revealed something I'd never known—*the only lasting way to the other side of shattering heartbreak is right through the dark valley, one step at a time.* I wish someone had told me the deep sorrow, confusion, and grief-related anxiety would not last forever!

If you've ever lost someone you love—whether there was time to prepare or their death came with no time to brace— you probably realize grief is one of the hardest things we ever face. That's why I wrote *Uncrushed: real steps for healing your grief and restoring your joy.* My hope is for Uncrushed to be a comforting place to...

- feel the emotions, rather than trying to numb them

- remember your loved one by writing about their life
- lean into the healing promises in God's word
- anticipate loving your life again and the possibility of finding a new purpose on the other side

Section One

Am I Okay?

Chapter One

Mom, You Don't Look Pretty Anymore!

O ur eleven-year-old daughter, Amy, needed a quick trip to Wilson's Five and Dime for a school project. We loved wandering the fabulously cluttered aisles of Wilson's, but today was different.

"Not today," I told her. "Maybe another time? I don't feel too great."

Amy fired back. "Mom, you don't look pretty anymore. You need to get a shower and put on some makeup and a cute outfit. Just because Beazy's not your mom anymore doesn't mean you don't need to be my mom."

Amy immediately started crying and apologized for her insensitive comment, but she was right. Since my mother, Beazy's sudden and crushing death, I had become a different person.

Where was the annoyingly optimistic mom my kids used to have? The one who delighted in finger painting with chocolate pudding and who laughed 'til she cried?

I didn't know where that mom was, and I wasn't sure if she was ever coming back.

The first weeks after my mom's graduation to Heaven were heartwarming, but a little confusing. Would our home be forever filled with Gerber daisies, homemade chicken pies, and friends sharing stories about her? Maybe this grief thing wouldn't be so terrible after all.

But as the days slowly marched on, friends and family returned to their own lives, and the anesthesia of their company wore off. Thanksgiving and Christmas were just weeks away, and the thought of the holidays without Beazy was unimaginable. The reality of living without my number-one cheerleader was paralyzing.

What do I do with this kind of pain? That and many other questions were running through my mind...

- Will the tsunami of tears ever end?
- Why do some people seem to skate through sorrow while I feel isolated and stuck?
- If my brain is this foggy and I'm contemplating hibernating 'til springtime, am I going crazy? Or is this what grief looks like?
- Where are the people who came around in the early days? Do they even care about me? Or about her?
- I wish I could have seen her sparkling blue eyes and said goodbye one last time. Where do I go with all the regrets?
- What if I forget about her one day?
- *Is God really able to heal my shattered heart?*

Dear friend, if you're reading this, I'm guessing you're missing an important part of your life puzzle. Whether you had time to say goodbye or death came suddenly, life without someone you love can feel chaotic, confusing, and downright crushing.

While every person's experience after loss is unique, you too may have more questions than answers. I don't know what you're going through, but I do know that when you care deeply about someone, the sorrow when they're gone can be overwhelming.

Through losing my mom, my dad, my very cool grandmom Nana, and my "yes-you-may-drive-my-purple-dune-buggy-to-high-school" sister-in-law, Kay, the Lord has reminded me that their life stories are absolutely too important and too rich to be forgotten.

One memorable story that comes to mind right now is the day my five-year-old brother, John, carved, with his kindergarten scissors on Mom's mahogany dining room table, "I LOVE MOMY." He didn't even spell her name right! While the tiny criminal got in a little trouble, everyone always knew Mom loved John's permanent love note.

> *Deep down we always understood that to Beazy, people were more important than things. Always.*

Deep down we always understood that to Beazy, people were more important than things. Always.

John has the permanent-love-note mahogany table in his dining room today. Little criminal.

I'm sharing this story, and a few more to come, because I believe you, too, have memories that are too important to be forgotten! Preserving priceless stories can be a significant step toward healing your grief and restoring your joy.

Wherever you are on your journey, will you imagine a few possible scenarios with me?

- What if the pain won't always be this intense?
- What if you could be confident that your loved one won't be forgotten?
- What if you're stronger than you think you are?
- What if the person who used to finger paint with chocolate pudding (or whatever your life used to look like) is still inside, anxious to return?
- What if God really can turn your mourning into dancing?

My friend, God sees you and He loves you. He will be with you every step of the way. No pain is too deep for Him to touch.

What if you could take real steps today toward healing your grief and restoring your joy-filled life?

I invite you to walk with me as we start the journey—not around the sorrow, but right through it.

The Lord has shown me over and over that He really is close to the brokenhearted. He really does rescue us when we're crushed in spirit (Psalm 34:18). *And it really is possible to become uncrushed!*

> *My friend, God sees you and He loves you. He will be with you every step of the way. No pain is too deep for Him to touch.*

My prayer is that these pages will be a sweet place to reflect and to write about the person you're missing.

Lord, please do what only You can do.
Restore Your sweet peace and joy in this dear one's life.
Amen.

Chapter Two

When Grief Feels Like Crazy

G rowing up in my big family, we were allowed to do some very cool things as kids. I'll never forget the day we piled two parents and five high-spirited kids into the station wagon, along with dad's shoebox of folded atlas maps. Our six-week pop-up camper trip began in Atlanta, with the destination of sunny California. The absolute highlight, besides the Grand Canyon and Disneyland, was the one night each week when we'd stay in a Howard Johnson's Motor Lodge.

We were always thrilled to see the familiar blue and orange retro neon sign on the horizon.

Late one night, somewhere in Arizona, while our parents slept soundly next door, we made the most magnificent discovery. Room service. Who knew you could have cheeseburgers, French fries, and HoJo's chocolate ice cream in fancy bowls delivered right to your hotel room?

As you might imagine, the party ended at checkout the next morning when our dad got the bill for our shenanigans. He was not amused, but I imagine he secretly wished he'd been invited to the excitement.

In our predominantly fun childhood, the one thing kids were never allowed to do was to participate in the arrangements when someone passed away. *Grief and sadness were simply not on the agenda.* When someone died, my brothers, sisters, and I would keep playing kickball and jumping on the trampoline, while our parents did funeral things. After the service, we rarely talked about their day or about the person who had died. Even in the years that followed, we didn't do much to remember our beloved family members who were now gone.

> *Shielding kids from sorrow is a big mistake, and it can create confusion and cluelessness around death and loss.*

As an adult, I learned quickly that shielding kids from sorrow is a big mistake, and it can create confusion and cluelessness around death and loss.

The unfamiliar, unpleasant emotions felt a lot like crazy to me. I had no idea if the deep sadness, the lack of desire to be around humans, or the inability to stop crying were normal parts of grieving.

Was it normal to feel…

- foggy, exhausted, and anxious?
- physical pain, like an elephant is standing on your chest?
- icky, like you have the flu?
- tearful and fearful of melting down in public?
- tired, but unable to sleep?
- restless, but unable to wake up?

Is This Crazy? Or Is It Grief?

The pain of my best friend/mom Beazy's sudden death left me with an anxiety like I had never known before. I was fearful that if someone mentioned her name in public, the tsunami of tears would start all over again, and it might never stop. If I had enough faith, I should be able to power through this grief thing by myself, right? When kind friends asked how I was doing, I'd smile and say, "Oh, I'm fine. We don't need anything."

But maybe it was time to quit being so stubborn and to let someone in.

I wasn't looking for another psychobabble-filled book, describing predictable stages of grief that I could expect, as if the journey would be neat and linear.

What I needed was for someone to tell me, "Girl, you're gonna make it through this. It will be a wild ride, but hold on tight. People want to help you. Let them. You've got what it takes."

> *What I needed was for someone to tell me, "Girl, you're gonna make it through this. It will be a wild ride, but hold on tight. People want to help you. Let them. You've got what it takes."*

Healthy Grief Rhythms

Last week when my friend Sharie received the unexpected call about her dad's death, she seemed to instinctively know how to let people into her pain instead of pretending everything was okay. Even though her dad's health had been declining, the news still came as a shock and left her with lots of questions about the days ahead. I loved the way Sharie—even in the early hours after receiving the news—started taking healthy steps toward healing her grief without even knowing it.

Here are a few Instagram posts Sharie shared in the days following her dad's death:

- "I lost my Dad today. I wish so many things could have been different in these last years with him. I had so many hopes and plans: to fish and ride in boats together, to learn to play golf (or at least try), to sit on a dock at the beach and listen to stories…"
- "A part of me is afraid to grieve, another part of me knows I need it. So I'm praying for acceptance for the joy and pain I will journey through as I learn how to heal from something which is completely unknown and unfamiliar."
- "Dad loved a good story and loved to teach—*it was his love currency.* You knew he loved you if he taught you how to do something—so we listened."
- "Our family had Dad's memorial service today. Waves of joy, peace, sadness, energy and tiredness are flowing through me. I'll just receive them as they come, giving myself grace for every emotion." —Sharie King

Sharie is a wise one. She already knows the importance of giving herself "grace for every emotion." Her natural desire to talk about her dad's life and share photos of happier days will surely give her strength in the days to come.

Because of her honesty in writing about what she's feeling, Sharie has already experienced an outpouring of prayer, kindness, and love as she starts the journey of life without her dad. She understands she's not going crazy. She's grieving.

How about You?

If you were allowed to experience sorrow and grief when you were growing up, you probably understood that dying is a natural part of life. Hopefully, you realized unpredictable emotions might come but would ultimately subside. You likely knew it was okay to feel whatever you were feeling *and that you were not going crazy. You were, and are, grieving.*

I wish someone like Sharie had been around when I started losing some of my favorite family people on earth!

I invite you to reflect and write about the way grief, mourning, and sorrow were integrated into your life during your childhood and adolescence. How did your family's grief habits shape how you're coping today? There's absolutely no pressure to write, but even a few words will be a wonderful starting place for the Lord to begin to do what only He can do—heal your heart.

Beth Marshall

_____

_____

_____

_____

_____

_____

_____

_____

_____

_____

_____

_____

_____

_____

_____

_____

_____

_____

_____

Chapter Three

Taking Off Your Superhero Cape

What used to feel like a steady and stable life can suddenly seem chaotic after the death of someone close. If you are more comfortable being the strong one who helps others through tangled times of trauma, your life might feel pretty messy right now.

When I was blindsided by my mom's death, I didn't have the slightest clue what this new unwelcome guest (grief) was supposed to look or feel like—or how long it would be staying.

I had always quietly wondered, "What's the big deal? How hard can it be to navigate life after loss?" That was before becoming a motherless daughter and losing my number-one cheerleader and life-hero, my mom.

Over the years, thanks to a snow skiing crash, hiking on a slippery slope in Alaska, and a less-than-graceful wipeout over my husband's barbell, I've managed to break three legs. You seriously can't make this stuff up. Note to self—whenever your teenaged or grown kids challenge you to participate in an extreme sport, it's okay to *just say no.*

After each leg mishap, orthopedic surgeons quickly

discerned the fractures could not just be reset. That would have been a whole lot quicker and easier, in my opinion. These busted appendages would need surgery, therapy, rest, and a whole lot of time to heal.

I'm not sure what made me think recovery from a shattered heart would require anything less. For some reason, I thought I should be able to power through the debilitating darkness, upside-down emotions, and extreme heartache without any help. Maybe it was my foolish pride, but for the first twelve months, I mistakenly thought this badly broken heart would heal on its own. In my opinion, I didn't need anybody.

> *Had I made the same stubborn decision with my orthopedic catastrophes, I'd probably still be frozen in the snow somewhere in Utah, unable to walk.*

Had I made the same stubborn decision with my orthopedic catastrophes, I'd probably still be frozen in the snow somewhere in Utah, unable to walk.

My determination to get through this life-changing loss all by myself was disastrous, not only for my life but also for the people I loved the most.

If I had it to do over, I would do things differently. I would…

- **quit lying when people asked how I was doing.** I would take a deep breath and tell the truth. "Actually, today is a really hard day. I'm hanging out alone at home so I don't run into anyone and start crying again."

- **stop saying, "I'm fine."** Miles Adcox, founder of Onsite counseling center, uses a humorous acronym for when we say we're "F.I.N.E."—Freaked Out, Insecure, Neurotic, and Emotional. For me, that was not too far from the truth.
- **let people love me.** There are probably people in your life—like there are in mine—who would genuinely do whatever they could to make things a little better when we're struggling—bring a warm meal, help with the kids, do yard work, provide financial coaching, you name it. Even when it feels awkward, I'd get into the habit of saying yes to support, companionship, a complimentary Caribbean cruise (I mean, why not?), or whatever useful help was offered.
- **talk with a pastor, friend, or a close family member.** Let them know I'm struggling and need help.
- **recognize that feeling sad is not a sign of weakness.** It's a normal part of grieving. It's okay to cry, shout, laugh, scream, and feel whatever I'm feeling.

Revelation 21:4, NLT is a powerful image of the day to come when *"He will wipe every tear from their eyes, and there will be no more death or sorrow or crying or pain. All these things are gone forever."*

How about You?

If you're trying to climb this mountain of pain all by yourself, dear friend, you don't have to. We were never intended to go through life's hardest times without love, support, and practical help from others.

What is something you could do today to get the help you need? Maybe you could phone a friend or check out a grief support group close by. If your grief is fresh, you may have no idea what you need. Goodness, I understand how that feels.

If there are people offering to do things for you, would you consider designating a **point person?** A point person is someone who can coordinate meals, carpooling, childcare, or whatever you need. This friend could organize all kinds of helpful goodness and get it on your calendar and off your plate.

Sometimes, healing means taking off our Superman/Superwoman cape for a season and allowing friends to step in and take some of the heavy burden we're carrying. It's okay. Hopefully, you'll be there for them one day when they need you.

"Praise be to the God and Father of our Lord Jesus Christ, the Father of compassion and the God of all comfort, who comforts us in all our troubles, so that we can comfort those in any trouble with the comfort we ourselves receive from God" (2 Corinthians 1:3-4, NIV).

This space is for writing whatever is on your mind today.

Uncrushed

Chapter Four

Comparison Is a Punk

"Comparison is a punk. It'll rip you off every single time." Thank you, Bob Goff.

You may be wondering if your trauma, tragedy, or adversity is more or less significant than someone else's. Maybe you're feeling stuck and confused while other people seem to coast through their grief.

My maternal grandmom, Nana, was a sassy one—strong and independent. Nana was a nursing supervisor back in the day. She was the classiest woman I'd ever seen when she'd leave for work in her starched white uniform and nurse hat. One of my favorite memories as a young child was spending a night away from my big family (five kids, two parents, and two crazy canines) with just Nana and me. There was nothing like her undivided attention, card games with just the two of us, and waking up to sunny-side-up "dippy" eggs and biscuits from a can. Life with Nana was grand!

Sadly, when Nana was in her nineties, her health began to decline, and we sensed that her days on this side of Heaven were numbered. I'll never forget going through the Atlanta airport on a trip, working for Delta Air Lines, when a supervisor met me in the jetway with some not shocking, but really hard news—I needed to call home. Nana had passed away. It's been twenty-five years now, and I'm still getting teary thinking about that day.

When I called my mom, she asked if I was okay to drive to her house. I assured her that I was just fine. After all, Nana was ninety-two, and we knew this day would come. But what happened next took me by surprise. As I started the familiar twenty-five minute drive to my mom's house just north of Atlanta, before I knew it, the interstate signs indicated I was heading south and would ultimately end up in Florida. Sometimes when painful news comes, we think our mind is clearer than it actually is. The death of a dear person in your life is a big deal. People sometimes make us feel that losing an older person, someone who's been in a long battle with illness, or someone with special needs somehow shouldn't be as hard as other losses.

> *The truth is, nobody had your exact relationship with your person. Your story and your grief are real and unique. Their life mattered. You deserve to be seen and heard, no matter who it is you're missing!*

The truth is, nobody had your exact relationship with your person. Your story and your grief are real and unique. Their life mattered. You deserve to be seen and heard, no matter who it is you're missing!

Did I Mention that Comparison Is a Punk?

Several years after losing my close loved ones, I was invited to lead a breakout session at a Hope for the Holidays grief support event. The room was filled to capacity with 250 people who were each experiencing fresh loss.

The tables were beautifully decorated with autumn flowers, and the well-dressed keynote speaker looked like a true pro. He even arrived with a personal videographer to record his every word.

The scene surrounding the confident motivational speaker appeared perfect…until he opened his mouth.

"Thank you so much for being here today. I just want you to know that whatever you're going through, there's somebody else who is going through something worse."

You could have heard a pin drop, as his insensitive opening remark covered the room in a dark cloud. The bereaved guests had mustered up the courage to show up, expecting to find understanding and compassion. Instead, their sorrow was compared and minimized, and it felt as though their loss was somehow not valid.

How about You?

Maybe you've been made to feel that what you're going through doesn't matter. Or that, because your person…

- had lived a full life
- was a stepfamily member or in-law
- had been sick a long time

...or for whatever reason, you shouldn't feel the way you feel.

Do you ever compare your grief journey with someone who seems stronger or more together than you? I surely have. But our loving Lord is not in the business of comparing what He created. We shouldn't be either.

I invite you to use these pages to write about any comparisons you've experienced around your grief.

Beth Marshall

Uncrushed

Chapter Five

With a Little Help from My Friends

T ime alone is essential when processing the unexpected emotions after loss. A steady diet of alone time, though, can lead to isolation. And the enemy of your soul loves to convince you that you don't need anybody. His strategy is to get you all alone so he can sneak in with his conniving, confusing voice whispering,

- "Where are all the cards and flowers and friends now?"
- "Nobody cares about you!"
- "Nobody cared about your person."
- "Your life will always be a 'griefy' mess."
- "Don't tell anyone you're struggling. They'll think you're weak!"

I wish I'd known, in my early months after loss, that admitting you can't handle something on your own is actually what strong people do.

What Not to Do

> *I wish I'd known, in my early months after loss, that admitting you can't handle something on your own is actually what strong people do.*

After my mom's death, I hunkered down all by myself for months and months. I had no idea how helpful it would have been to invite people into the pain. In that place of solitude isolation, I started to believe the lies (see above) about what I was going through, and how long it might last. I started thinking not only that nobody cared about me but also that nobody cared about my mom. Fear crept in, and I wondered if this dark unfamiliar cave of sorrow might be my new permanent residence.

I now understand that it didn't have to be that way.

Things that Help

Sometimes you just need someone to show up and be a safe, loving space where you can feel what you feel.

A friendly face, a shoulder to cry on—if you feel like crying—and a listening ear can be more comforting than hours on a psychiatrist's couch. A trusted friend who understands your pain will help you feel seen and heard and remind you that you are not alone.

> *Sometimes you just need someone to show up and be a safe, loving space where you can feel what you feel.*

Even though we "walk through

the valley of the shadow of death," we were never intended to set up camp there or call it our forever home.

Do you have someone in your life who won't tap out when things get rough? Someone who cares for you and knows how to show up, without having to speak a lot of words?

Finding Your People

Goodness, I wish someone had whispered, "Girl, you don't have to go through this alone." I wish I had known about the countless groups that exist solely to offer relief and companionship in grief.

> *Even though we "walk through the valley of the shadow of death," we were never intended to set up camp there or call it our forever home.*

Now, thanks to the internet, online grief-relief organizations have sprung up around the world to offer compassionate support along our journeys.

A few years ago, a lovely group called Motherless Daughters was created in Australia to support and connect girls who had lost their "mum" at a young age. They bring "expertise, shared experiences and a unique perspective on one of life's most precious and enduring relationships."

This caring organization offers online and in-person communities for women of all ages to "comfort, soothe and support each other in a non-judgmental space." How cool is that concept? Gracious, I wish these ladies had been around when I became a motherless daughter.

The Compassionate Friends is another outstanding

outreach for moms, dads, sisters, brothers, grandparents, friends, and basically anyone who is grieving the death of a child (at any age, from any cause). This phenomenal non-profit organization offers friendship, understanding, and hope for heartbroken families.

"Some of us are far along in our grief, but others still feel a grief so fresh and so intensely painful that they feel helpless and see no hope. Some of us have found our faith to be a source of strength, while others struggle to find answers. Some of us are angry, filled with guilt or in deep depression, while others radiate an inner peace. But whatever pain we bring to this gathering of The Compassionate Friends, it is pain we will share, just as we share with each other our love for the children who have died. [. . .] We reach out to each other in love to share the pain as well as the joy, share the anger as well as the peace, share the faith as well as the doubts, and help each other to grieve as well as to grow. We Need Not Walk Alone." —The Compassionate Friends

How about You?

Whether you prefer spending time with an individual or connecting with a group, please know you don't have to go through profound loss alone.

What are your thoughts around getting a little help? Is there someone you could text or call on a particularly hard day? If you are comfortable with social media, Facebook and Instagram can be excellent places to connect with others who genuinely understand what you're feeling.

These pages are for writing any thoughts you have, or specific names of individuals or groups you might reach out to for support if you're feeling overwhelmed, anxious, or isolated.

_____

_____

_____

_____

_____

_____

_____

_____

_____

_____

_____

_____

_____

_____

_____

_____

_____

_____

_____

_____

_____

Chapter Six

Rx Meds, Amazon Prime, and M&Ms
Help for a Minute...'Til They Don't

There are countless creative ways we attempt to numb the pain after loss. Whether our drug of choice is Rx meds, mindless media, alcohol, busyness, food, shopping, or something else, sadly, reality returns the moment the high wears off. Sometimes reality returns with even more intensity. So what do you do when the sorrow comes back?

If you've ever had scary dental work done, feeling the novocaine starting to take effect is heavenly.

Dentist: "Is it numb yet?"

Me: "Not quite. Let's wait a little longer."

Dentist: "How about now?"

Me: "Ummmm, maybe three more minutes."

Can anyone else relate?

The weeks following the life-shattering call about my mom's death were filled with family, friends, food, flowers, frantic activity, and quite honestly, I was in a haze of shock. As the temporary numbing started to wear off and reality set in,

I realized what a rookie griever I was. In fact, this was my first experience on the front row of a funeral.

I wish I could say I turned to all the healthy habits to manage the sorrow, but in reality, I was grabbing for anything that might distract my mind and heart, even for a moment, from feeling what had just happened.

> *The person who knew everything about me, and somehow loved me anyway, was gone—and I had no idea how to keep going.*

The person who knew everything about me, and somehow loved me anyway, was gone—and I had no idea how to keep going.

Here are a few things that helped me for a minute…'til they didn't:

- **busyness.** Maybe if I moved fast enough and broke up all the flower arrangements into small vases and delivered them all over town, people would think I was super generous and that I was coping really well. Maybe the pain couldn't catch me.
- **medication.** Scrounging through the medicine cabinet for Rx sleeping aids helped…'til the pills ran out three days later. Sidenote: If medication is prescribed to help you cope with the trauma of loss, that's another story. You and your doctor know best.
- **shopping.** One more colorful dress would certainly brighten my mood, right?
- **delicious food.** Homemade chicken pie was delightful and comforting, but when the last tasty morsel

was gone, all that remained was a full belly, a dirty casserole dish, and an empty heart.

- **mindless entertainment.** Movies and TV were entertaining, 'til the distraction no longer helped.

I wish someone had told me that temporary fixes feel good in the moment, but long-term, there had to be a better way.

I wish I had known there were healthier ways to face sorrow. Things like…

- slowing down and feeling what I was actually feeling
- not apologizing for being sad
- saying her name and encouraging others to do the same
- realizing that it's okay to cry, even in public
- taking time every day to be still, cry, pray, scream, sleep, or do whatever I needed to do
- asking someone to pray for and with me
- considering the possibility that God really could turn my mourning into dancing

> *I wish someone had told me that temporary fixes feel good in the moment, but long-term, there had to be a better way.*

"You have turned my mourning into joyful dancing. You have taken away my clothes of mourning and clothed me with joy, that I might sing praises to you and not be silent." Psalm 30:11-12a, NLT

How about You?

Maybe you have a wonderful arsenal of healthy grieving techniques. But if not, you may have turned to things that helped ease the ache momentarily, but long-term, didn't enable healing.

These pages are a great place to write about what has or hasn't helped you in moving forward through your grief journey. This is a safe place to be honest. These pages are for your eyes only, unless you decide to share them with a dear friend, a family member, or maybe a counselor. It's never too late to open up.

Beth Marshall

_____

_____

_____

_____

_____

_____

_____

_____

_____

_____

_____

_____

_____

_____

_____

_____

_____

_____

_____

_____

_____

_____

_____

_____

_____

_____

_____

_____

_____

_____

_____

_____

_____

_____

_____

_____

Section Two

What Am I Afraid Of?

Chapter Seven

"Okay, Everybody Smile!" and More Ridiculous Things People Say

Hundreds had gathered in our small town to honor a respected businessman. The family's matriarch was preparing to walk into the funeral for her beloved husband of fifty-plus years. Suddenly, she turned around, clapped her hands, and gave the family their marching orders. As aunts, uncles, sisters, and brothers prepared to enter the church sanctuary, she said, "Okay, everybody smile!"

People say some pretty unusual things—helpful things, not-so-helpful things, and some downright chuckle-worthy things in the awkward days after loss. It's okay to laugh, and it's okay to cry. Smiling is good for the soul.

"Laughter is carbonated holiness." —*Anne Lamott*

Ridiculous Remarks

If you're one of the rare individuals who knows exactly what to say when someone's heart has been broken, I'm thankful for you. The other ninety-nine percent of the world, myself included, will occasionally make an insensitive or hurtful remark when trying to fill an uncomfortable silence.

Maybe you've been told how, at least…

- You're young. You'll marry again.
- You can have more kids.
- They died quickly and you didn't have to watch them suffer.
- They're in a better place.

Or maybe someone tried to assure you that…

- Time heals all things.
- They wouldn't want you to be sad.
- Everything happens for a reason.
- You should be "over it" by now.

And the gold medal for what to not say to a griever… "So I guess God needed another little angel." Seriously?! In the words of my brilliant friend Tara-Leigh Cobble, the angel comment is, "a theological disaster, biblically inaccurate, and (even if you don't believe scripture) it's dismissive. Instead, you could just say you really loved that person and will miss them."

Dear friend, if I was ever the one who tried to make sense of your tragedy, or whispered, even without saying a word, that it's time to move on—please forgive me. For the times someone assumed your heart shouldn't still be aching for your dear person, no matter how long it's been—I'm sorry they didn't understand. If your feelings felt squashed by someone attempting to hurry up your healing, that had to be hurtful.

A Few Words that Helped

"I wish there was something I could say to ease your heartache, but please know I'm not going anywhere."

"I'm so sorry you're going through this pain. Don't forget, I'm just a call away—and it's never too early or too late to call. I'll be right there."

"The thing I loved most about your mom was…"

Scripture Bombs

If someone has ever dropped a passage of scripture on you, attempting to make things better after a dear loved one has died and it felt strange to you…you are not alone.

Just because words are in the Bible—and are true—doesn't mean they will always be the most helpful message in the wake of crushing loss.

One great example of misused scripture comes from Romans *8:28, NIV. "And we know that in all things God works for the good of those who love him, who have been called according to his purpose."*

Just because words are in the Bible—and are true—doesn't mean they will always be the most helpful message in the wake of crushing loss.

These words are absolutely true, and I'm eternally grateful for their profound truth. However, dropping this particular passage on someone whose heart has just been shattered can minimize how they're feeling right *now*.

What Friends Do

"They share the pain, and they shut up. They don't give pious platitudes. They don't give advice. They don't try to talk a friend out of his pain. They don't say, 'It's going to be okay.' They just say, 'We're going to sit here with you. We're going to be here for you." —Pastor Rick Warren after the death of his beloved son, Matthew

James 1:19, NIV offers timeless wisdom to *"be quick to listen, slow to speak, and slow to become angry."*

I'm not trying to drop a scripture bomb here, but I do love how these wise words offer insight for anyone (preaching to myself here) needing to take a deep breath before attempting to say something brilliant or profound.

Ridiculous Things I've Said

My mouth said: Hey—so sorry I didn't get back to you.

While my mind thought: *But I really don't feel like talking to or seeing any humans right now. In all honesty, I'd rather take a nap. Or watch another Netflix series. Or eat some dark chocolate. I hear it's good for your heart. This grief thing is knocking me out. I had no idea it would fill every single corner of my life. And how is the entire planet carrying on, going to work, meeting for coffee, laughing and smiling, as though nothing happened, while my life feels like a dumpster fire? I was thinking about returning your call, but my phone is turned off, because what if somebody calls with more bad news?*

Then my mouth said: I'm good. How are you?

How about You?

I invite you to use these pages to record whatever comes to mind:

- a comment that was so preposterous, it actually made you chuckle
- a time when you were slightly less than truthful when a trusted person attempted to check in on you
- a passage of scripture, dropped at a not-very-helpful time, and how it made you feel
- a passage of scripture that actually was comforting

_____

_____

_____

_____

_____

_____

_____

_____

_____

_____

_____

_____

_____

_____

_____

_____

_____

_____

_____

Chapter Eight

Missed Milestones

When a loved one dies, the fear of facing what's right now is hard enough, but the fear of facing future milestones without them can feel impossible. Taking the time to acknowledge missed milestones can help you prepare your heart and mind for facing events in the future without your person.

Even though my sister-in-love Kay has been gone for over five years, whenever I see her precious grandkids, I'm reminded how she would have loved seeing them explore the world with curiosity and wonder. Whether it's a birthday, kindergarten graduation, baptism, or wedding, our family includes Kay's name. We talk about her and dream about what she might be thinking or might say on this special day, if she were still with us.

Here are a few ideas for how to spend a difficult milestone day:

- Understand that the anticipation before the day may be tougher than the actual day.

- Be real. Journal, write, call someone who may also be struggling on this important day.
- Do what your person loved to do. Eat their favorite meal.
- Allow yourself to lean into what you're feeling—sad, anxious, exhausted, relieved, joyful, whatever it is.
- Call or visit a friend or family member who is also struggling with the loss. Tell and retell favorite stories.
- Be honest at work, home, and with friends. When someone you trust asks how you're doing, take a deep breath and tell the truth. Let them know this is your first, or whatever number, holiday season since losing someone dear in your life.
- Spend the day volunteering with a charity that was important to your person. Reaching out to serve others can combat loneliness on a difficult day.
- Plant something—a tree or perennial plant in their memory.
- Host a dinner party and ask guests to bring their favorite comfort food.

> *Whether you spend the day surrounded by others, or by yourself under a cozy comforter watching I Love Lucy reruns, being kind to yourself is always a great idea.*

Whether you spend the day surrounded by others, or by yourself under a cozy comforter watching *I Love Lucy* reruns, being kind to yourself is always a great idea.

One of the best ways to prepare for a tough milestone day

on the horizon is to let friends—both in real life and on social media—know the big day is coming. Invite them to walk the day out with you.

Use these pages to write about milestones, how they affect you, and what you might do to prepare for a day that's coming up soon. There is no right or wrong way to approach a hard anniversary. Stirring up memories gives young children a clearer image of the person you're all missing, more than a one-dimensional photo ever could.

Uncrushed

_____

_____

_____

_____

_____

_____

_____

_____

_____

_____

_____

_____

_____

_____

_____

_____

_____

_____

_____

_____

Beth Marshall

Chapter Nine

Afraid of Not Being Okay—Josh's Story

Deep loss can lead to days when you're really not okay, and that's okay. My friends Josh and Tayla know all too well what crushing grief feels like.

Josh and Tayla are two of my favorites. They're pretty easy to pick out in a crowd, thanks to their endearing Aussie accents, Josh's standing of six-feet-eight-inches tall, and Tayla's smile that could light up the night sky. Three years ago, this lovely twentysomething couple left their homeland on the Gold Coast of Australia for a new ministry opportunity 9,500 miles away—in the upstate of South Carolina. Seriously, who does that?

Moving away from most everything they knew and loved had to be one of the toughest decisions ever, but these two were all in for the challenge. It's no surprise this lovable couple from down under was quickly embraced by friends they now consider their American family.

But nothing could have prepared Josh and Tayla for the most shocking ten words of their lives. Four days before Christmas, the crushing news from Josh's dad came with no warning: "Josh, I'm so sorry, but your mum didn't wake up." Josh's full-of-life, healthy forty-eight-year-old mum, Jo, had died suddenly during the night, as a result of an apparent "random heart valve collapse."

Josh describes the pain as "piercing, like someone stabbing me in the heart." As the shock of his mum's death began to sink in, he remembers two dear friends arriving at his door with dinner from a favorite local restaurant. The friends didn't try to craft brilliant words to make things better or attempt to fix anything. They just showed up to do what dear friends do—sit with Josh and Tayla in their sorrow.

On the long flights home, Josh experienced a crippling thought: *What if he forgot about his beloved mum?* He started to write through the tears. For hours and hours, Josh wrote in his journal everything he could possibly remember about her. He recorded memories of coming home after school, knowing she would be there with a snack, homework help, arts and crafts, and endless adventures. Josh describes his mum as "full of love, faithfulness" and "strict in the right ways." Jo was deeply committed to family and prioritized sweet time around the table at family dinners.

On Christmas Day, Josh and his family sat together, overlooking the stunning Gold Coast. For hours, they shared memories through lots of tears, but their grief was also laced with great joy. They experienced deep peace and thankfulness, even in the midst of their unthinkable sorrow, as the family celebrated the remarkable woman they called their mum.

The thought of going back to South Carolina was a difficult one. Josh felt torn between returning to the US to the thriving ministry he loved and staying in Australia to offer caring support for his family. As they scattered Jo's ashes, Josh's dad assured him that he and Josh's sisters would be okay. He gently reminded Josh, "We're so proud of you."

A Gift from God

In the months following Jo's death, Josh took some time to process his grief at a beautiful sanctuary in South Carolina, The Potter's Place. This lovely wooded property sprinkled with prayer cabins is a haven for weary pastors—a safe place to be still, rest, pray, and hear from the Lord. Josh remembers asking the Lord that day, "What does this year hold for me?" In the quiet moments, Josh sensed the Lord whisper, "Life from death."

He wasn't sure exactly what "life from death" meant until the one-year anniversary of his mum's death. It was a difficult day, but one Josh and Tayla will forever cherish, as they sat in the doctor's office celebrating the twenty-week ultrasound image of their beloved son, Elijah.

While Josh still misses his mum more than words can say, he has a unique ability to embrace the deep sadness and profound gratefulness simultaneously. In his words, "I had a front row seat to an incredible woman."

"She taught me generosity, and how to open my home and be hospitable...shaping my life as a potter and clay."

> *"She taught me generosity, and how to open my home and be hospitable... shaping my life as a potter and clay."*

As their precious baby boy grows up, Josh is grateful that his mum's loving, kind, godly DNA will always be part of Elijah's life. "I get the privilege of carrying on her legacy and knowing I'll forever be her boy." He added, "I'm filled with deep joy and gratitude knowing we will be reunited again. One day, soon enough."

Josh currently leads hundreds of young men and women, ages 18 to 25, across the state of South Carolina in the Rally Ministry of NewSpring Church. One of the healthiest ways Josh continues to heal is by sharing his grief journey with those he serves. His vulnerability says to the young adults that there's no shame in expressing the hard emotions and that deep restorative healing and great purpose really are possible, even after unimaginable loss.

Some of the healthy steps Josh has taken through the grief process are...

- talking and writing openly about his mum
- crying when he needs to cry
- knowing it's okay to ask questions
- leaning into his faith
- preserving memories to share with their son, Elijah

"We are hard pressed on every side, but not crushed; perplexed, but not in despair; persecuted, but not abandoned; struck down, but not destroyed." 2 Corinthians 4:8-9, NIV

How about You?

Josh told me that since losing his mum, his faith has become more real than ever. Does that resonate with you? If not, that's okay too. Do you feel the freedom to ask questions when life doesn't make sense?

I invite you to use the following pages to write about anything that resonates with you about Josh's story. There's no need to tidy up your feelings. Write as raw and unfiltered as you want to. That's where the healing begins.

"God really is with you as the crushing subsides." —My friend, Josh Bull

Beth Marshall

_____

_____

_____

_____

_____

_____

_____

_____

_____

_____

_____

_____

_____

_____

_____

_____

_____

_____

Section Three

What about You?

Chapter Ten

When the Flowers Fade

I don't know what it's like in other cultures, but here in America when someone dies on a Thursday, our culture seems to whisper, "So you'll be back in the office on Monday, right?"

For some, jumping right back into work and life is the next right decision. Maybe your typical day—weeks after the funeral—includes going for a run, meeting up for dinner with friends, and planning your next vacation. That is awesome. Whatever feels right for you is right for you.

For others, the thought of trying to focus, make a decision, or be around other humans after deep loss feels impossible. A good day is more like taking a nap, remembering to get a shower by bedtime, and reminding yourself to breathe. Again, whatever feels right for you is right for you.

What I know is that mourning

> *For those wrestling through deep sorrow, several weeks after the service can feel as though life has returned to normal—for everybody but you!*

is hard—it takes time and can feel totally weird once the frenetic pace surrounding the death and a memorial service comes to a halt.

For those wrestling through deep sorrow, several weeks after the service can feel as though life has returned to normal—for everybody but you!

When the flowers have faded and the last morsel of homemade comfort food is gone, the world around you can get really quiet. The silence can be deafening. Doubt and insecurity may creep in as you wonder where everybody has gone.

When Friends Go Missing in Action

Here are a few thoughts @GriefKid shared on Instagram:

"'I didn't call because I figured you wanted to be alone.'
(But a call or text would have let me know for sure that I wasn't alone.)"

"'I was afraid of saying the wrong thing, so I didn't say anything.'
(But saying nothing, made me feel forgotten.)"

"'I told you to call if you need anything.'
(But, unfortunately, I don't know what I need right now.)"
—@GriefKid

"Rejoice with those who rejoice, weep with those who weep."
Romans 12:15, ESV

A friend who will sit with you in sorrow is a rare gift from the Lord.

Things that Helped

Even though reaching out after loss can feel awkward, here are a few practical yet inexpensive ideas grievers have shared. After my loved one died, someone...

- dropped off a basket of fruit and other healthy snacks
- dropped off a bag of burgers and fries, just in case the family was tired of fruit and healthy snacks :)
- offered to pick up the kids after school, then returned them at bedtime, bathed and fed
- sent an email gift card from a meal delivery company
- sent a note and included a fun memory and a photo of the person you lost.

However you speak love to a grieving family will probably be just the right thing to do.

Lovely words from a friend who didn't know your loved one.

I'm so sorry I didn't know your...(sister, father, whoever passed away), but based on who you are, ...(he/she) must have been...(you fill in the kind adjective).

Letting a griever know you wish you could have known their loved one will hopefully be appreciated.

Have you ever been told "your note, gift, call, text, prayer, or whatever you did, came at the exact right time"? That's because it's never the wrong time to reach out in kindness.

There's no greater gift than a story about a loved one at the moment it seems there will never be new stories.

How about You?

> *There's no greater gift than a story about a loved one at the moment it seems there will never be new stories.*

Were there people who inadvertently tried to microwave your grief process? Did anyone say something like, "Aren't you over this yet?"

Until someone has experienced intense loss, the kind that literally takes your breath away, it's impossible to understand what you may be feeling. This space is for reflecting and writing about the early days and weeks after your loss and how it made you feel when someone tried to rush you into "being your old self."

Beth Marshall

Uncrushed

Chapter Eleven

Help! I Need Somebody

I'll never forget the day, a few months after my mom's death, when for a split second I thought, "Why should I buckle my seatbelt? If that eighteen-wheel truck hit my car, all this pain would go away." This thought, although fleeting, was terrifying. I had no idea where to turn for help when the darkness became more than I could handle.

Waves of sorrow would hit when I least expected them. The minute my head hit the pillow at night, my mind would start racing with anxiety and worries about the future. The thought of being around people, especially crowds of people, felt paralyzing.

Every person's experience is unique, but the helplessness many feel can easily transition to a place of hopelessness. I wish someone had told me that the deep pit where I was camping would not be my forever home. I had no idea the debilitating sadness was only temporary. I wish someone had suggested getting professional help, but with my Academy Award–winning acting where I pretended I had it all under control, nobody knew how dark my world had become.

Month after month, I tried to convince everyone around me that I was FINE. Well, now I understand that "fine" is a four-letter word. Not the kind that gets you in trouble in middle school, but nevertheless, a dangerous word that can keep you anxious, isolated, and stuck.

Telling people you're good, when you're not, is like being in the middle of the ocean, and everyone but you has a lifeboat. As salty wave after salty wave takes you under, you desperately scramble to stay afloat, confident you don't need anybody or anything. Before long, you're all alone, way in over your head, and sinking fast.

> *I wish there was a "Handle with care—I'm grieving" t-shirt.*

I wish there was a "Handle with care—I'm grieving" t-shirt.

If you or someone you know is feeling life isn't worth living anymore, today's the day to seek immediate professional help. A family physician, pastor, or counselor can all be excellent starting places, if thoughts of suicide or hurting another person occur.

Have I Slipped under God's Radar?

When life feels out of control, someone you love is suffering, or a dear person in your life dies, it's not unusual for your faith to take a hit. Understandably, grief can leave you questioning God's goodness and His presence.

For over twenty years, my family somehow managed to steer clear of any major trauma, loss, or catastrophe. Floating through life when nothing rocks your boat is relatively easy. It's not 'til the waves start rolling in that you realize you're in over your head. It took my running out of all other options to figure out that what I needed was some serious divine intervention.

Here's a bit of my story.

Our first child, tiny baby Michael arrived just on time for his schedule, but four weeks ahead of his predicted ETA. The scrawny little guy would scream his ever-loving head off every two hours…all night long. Good thing he was cute and cuddly. At the same time, my parents were in the middle of a heartbreaking divorce. Remember the parents who took five kids camping for six weeks and were the most fun ever? Those parents.

This fiercely independent twenty-seven-year-old new mom had always been able to figure out pretty much everything on her own. Until now. The combination of watching my family collapse before my eyes while suffering from serious sleep deprivation was way more than I could handle.

I'll never forget the morning when, all alone in my cozy chair, I cried out, "Jesus, if You're real, I need You. Please come into my life. I can't do this by myself anymore."

I wish I could tell you the heavens immediately parted, glorious angels descended, and all the pain vanished. As you might imagine, that's not what happened. What did happen, though, was still pretty miraculous. When I woke the next morning, it felt as though a gentle rain had washed away some of the debilitating sadness and exhaustion.

> *"Jesus, if You're real, I need You. Please come into my life. I can't do this by myself anymore."*

My gut-wrenching prayer had been heard, and I knew for the first time I could remember that I was not alone.

Starting a relationship with the Lord felt awkward at first. Without much of a church background, I was thankful when a friend invited me to be part of a four-week study called *Ten Brave Christians.* The (sadly, no longer in print) plan suggested…

- waking up a little earlier than usual
- reading a couple Bible verses
- recording prayers in a journal

The table of contents in the Bible became my best friend. No judgment here. After thirtysomething years, the table of contents and I are still shamelessly good friends. In those quiet early morning moments, I slowly began to grasp how much God loved me, even through all the years when I tried navigating life without Him.

Through some of my most difficult days ever, I realized He was not only the Creator of the universe—which would have been one hundred percent awesome enough—but He was also a wonderful Counselor and the Prince of Peace. He was the exact kind of friend my fractured life craved.

If you've ever been through a painful season, and started to question your faith, I get it.

The phenomenal thing I've discovered is that you don't have to have everything figured out, or understand every word of the Bible, or have all the answers. I surely don't.

Starting a relationship with the Lord, thankfully, is much less complicated than I could have imagined. Which is great, because you probably aren't looking for more complications right now. If you haven't already, would you consider asking Him to walk with you, take away some of the pain, and begin to heal your heart? No pressure, but He really is able to hold and help you.

"If you declare with your mouth, 'Jesus is Lord,' and believe in your heart that God raised him from the dead, you will be saved." Romans 10:9, NIV

Remember Josh from chapter nine? Here is his simple, yet profound guide for spending time with God.

Time with God

Five Minutes—Slow Reading of Scripture
Pick one psalm to slowly read out loud.
Use this as a springboard for prayer.

Ten Minutes—Journal
Write out how you are honestly feeling.
Write what you're thankful for.
Hold nothing back.

Five Minutes—Silence
Focus on Jesus, but embrace the silence.
Let your soul breathe.

How about You?

In the wake of losing a dear person, it's not unusual to have doubts and lots of unanswered questions. Reaching out to a friend, pastor, or someone else you trust can help you to not feel so alone with questions around faith and grief.

Keep in mind...

When an imperfect person (like me) admits I can't do this by myself anymore, that's when the Perfect One (the Lord) will step in to walk with you. Forever.

Please use this space to write about any doubts, fears, or faith-related issues you might be experiencing. Your concerns are valid, and they matter. Writing your unfiltered questions is a great way to begin to process what you're going through.

Beth Marshall

Chapter Twelve

Swimming in Peanut Butter

My brave US military widow friend Fran once told me that since her hero's death, her life "feels like swimming in peanut butter." You may understand all too well what she's talking about. You walk into a room and turn around wondering why in the world you're there. You can't make a decision or come up with a common word you use all the time. Grief-related fogginess can lead to a fear of forgetting about your loved one.

Loss can make life feel chaotic. One of the best steps toward getting your life back and reclaiming a bit of control is to start reflecting on your unique memories—the good ones, the not-so-great ones, all of them.

My Dad

My dad was an actuary, which I understood to mean "an extraordinarily smart mathematical human." I believe the fact that he grew up as an only child gave him the superpower of patience when dealing with his five ultra-curious kids. The scent of office supplies—fresh pencils, his Xerox machine, and carbon paper (anyone remember that?)—was intoxicating to me. My brothers, sisters, and I could play for hours in his office building behind our house. There was nothing like double-checking our math homework with his vintage adding machine, the size of a Boeing 747.

Dad also loved an occasional smoke of his beautiful wooden tobacco pipe. Please don't judge. It was the 1960s when smoking was what cool people did. One particularly creative Saturday morning, I remember replacing the tobacco from his wooden pipe with bubbles. In what world would that have been a wise idea?

I quickly realized his sacred pipe was created for tobacco only, and my bubble caper was not as funny as I might have anticipated. I also knew deep down, as a child, that dad would never ever stop loving me or my brothers and sisters. That's the kind of unconditional crazy love I hope our kids and grandkids always feel from me.

A Different Kind of Grief

I wish I could tell you life was always fun and idyllic with my dad.

Sadly, in his mid-fifties, something changed. Something drastically changed

Instead of the tennis-playing, party-hosting, traveling-to-work-for-Lloyd's-of-London dad, he slowly turned into someone we couldn't recognize.

It all started with a series of sleepless nights, followed by some uncharacteristically quiet days. During this unforeseen season, our normally high-energy, extroverted dad would be found in a dark room with the curtains closed, working on a Rubik's Cube for hours and days on end. The sadness, hopelessness, and restlessness he experienced were impossible to understand.

I remember saying, "Dad, let's go for a run, or hit some tennis balls." Sports were what we loved doing together—but nothing could touch the dark valley he had set up camp in.

Then, with no warning, his mood could shift dramatically in the course of a few hours to a place of erratic behavior, making extravagant purchases, and displaying an aggression we had never seen before.

Sadly, the unpredictable manic episodes ultimately turned into violence against my precious mom, Beazy.

After several cycles of this pattern, Dad was diagnosed with manic depression. Later, his diagnosis was changed to bipolar disorder. The psychiatrist told him and the rest of our family that even though Dad would always require medication, the extreme mood swings were *entirely treatable.*

The most gut-wrenching part of the story is that Dad refused to take medication for this completely treatable situation.

The shrapnel from his decisions led to a painful collapse of his business, the death of his thirty-five-year marriage to my mom, and seeing our family crumble right before our eyes.

In the words of my brilliant

> *"Death is not the only way we lose our loved ones. Long before he died, you lost your father to severe mental illness."*
>
> —David Montgomery

cousin David, "Death is not the only way we lose our loved ones. Long before he died, you lost your father to severe mental illness."

Dear friend, I don't share this for sympathy. Please hear me when I say the Lord has done and continues to do miraculous healing in my heart. As I re-open this painful chapter, though, I'm realizing that even decades later, this complicated grief still needs more work. Maybe you understand what I'm talking about. Thankfully, it's never too late.

> *"Sometimes God lets you hit rock bottom*
> *so you will discover that He is the Rock*
> *at the bottom." —Dr. Tony Evans*

There are a couple things I hope you take away from the broken road my family has traveled.

1. Taking medication does not mean you are weak.

If you or someone you love has ever resisted treatment for their mental wellness, I get it. Sometimes we believe that if we have enough faith, we shouldn't need medication. What I've seen in my own life is that there are times when medication and therapy have been important parts of God's miraculous plan.

2. Sometimes forgiveness feels impossible.

"Be kind to one another, tenderhearted, forgiving one another, as God in Christ forgave you." Ephesians 4:32, ESV

But, Lord, do I have to?

I remember knowing deep down that I needed to find a way to forgive my dad for all the hurt his decisions had caused. The problem was, *I could not do it.*

One day, I literally cried out to God, "I can't forgive him." I remember hearing, not an audible voice, but nevertheless a very clear word, "That's right, you can't forgive him. But with Me, you can."

God gently revealed to me that my dad's father had battled his own demons, and that my loving dad would never ever have chosen this path. Over time, the Lord softened my heart and allowed me to fully forgive him.

Forgiveness did not say what he did wasn't horrific. But it allowed me to see him as a broken man, fighting a fierce battle in his mind that others could not see.

I understood that Dad still loved me with all his heart. Forgiveness allowed me to fully love him again too.

While there is no big bow at the end of this story, I am forever grateful that, after a fifteen-year struggle, *my beloved dad finally accepted treatment* and was able to rebuild his life, heal some of the shattered relationships, and regain much of what he had lost. Sadly, some relationships were never restored.

> *Forgiveness did not say what he did wasn't horrific. But it allowed me to see him as a broken man, fighting a fierce battle in his mind that others could not see.*

Those of us closest to him were able to see the kind, gentle man we adored come back—the dad who loved and cherished his five kids, put us all through braces, tennis lessons, and college. The same one who drove our mischievous crew across the country—dragging a

> *Healing begins when we bring all the broken pieces to the Lord.*

pop-up camper—and even paid for our room service escapades at the Howard Johnson's Motor Lodge. That dad.

How about You?

Have you ever felt like you were swimming in peanut butter, like my friend Fran and I have?

Whether your pain was caused by the loss of a relationship, the death of a dream, or life taking a turn you never saw coming—grief, in whatever form, is hard work.

I hope my family's real reel hasn't been too much for you. I also hope that if you're going through some kind of complicated grief, you're able to connect with some well-deserved help. As soon as this manuscript is turned in, that's my plan too.

Forgiveness changes everything.

Healing begins when we bring *all* the broken pieces to the Lord.

When we admit we can't do this on our own, He steps in and gently assures us, "You're right, you can't—but together we can."

Feel free to use this space to write whatever comes to mind.

Beth Marshall

Chapter Thirteen

Releasing Regrets and
Finding Forgiveness

After your loved one died, you may have been left with regrets—maybe from things you wish you had said, or things you wish you hadn't said. It's hard to keep moving, or even to sleep at night, with a relentless loop of regrets running through your mind.

Shaking Off the Shackles of Regret

How do you get started?

1. Call it out. Be specific and figure out exactly what it is you would have done differently if you had the chance.

For example...

"I regret that we never got to say goodbye."

"I'm so sad we had that silly fight."

"I can't believe the grandkids will never know their amazing grandmom."

2. Write it out. A journal is a wonderful and safe place to express what you might be reluctant to say out loud. Downloading your unfiltered thoughts—the good, bad, bitter, angry, confusing, and even relieved emotions—is phenomenal *free therapy.*

3. Give it up. Writing a letter to the person you're missing, or even a letter to God, can be an excellent step toward healing.

Sample Letter

Dear _____,

Goodness, losing you has taken the wind out of my sails. There are so many things I wish had happened differently.

If I had known (date) was going to be your last day here on earth, we would have never had that ridiculous argument. Now I can't even remember what it was about. Please forgive me if I started it.

I would have spent more time doing fun things with you and not been so serious all the time. We would have laughed more together, and I would have told you more often how much you mean to me.

Please know I will always miss you.

Beth

So what do you do with the letter? You could mail it to yourself, attach it to a balloon, and literally *let it go.* You might share it with a close friend, grief counselor, or support group. You could keep it in your journal to revisit in the future. The choice is yours.

Rehashing regrets will leave you discouraged, disillusioned, and downright stuck.

More Thoughts on Forgiveness

If there are things you need to forgive your loved one for—or maybe you're struggling to forgive yourself—here's an extraordinary resource:

Forgiving What You Can't Forget: Discover How to Move On, Make Peace with Painful Memories, and Create a Life That's Beautiful Again

In this timeless book, New York Times best-selling author, Lysa TerKeurst shares her real-life story of hurt, heartbreak, and betrayal, along with practical steps to start the difficult, yet doable process of forgiveness.

> *Rehashing regrets will leave you discouraged, disillusioned, and downright stuck.*

"It is necessary for you not to let pain rewrite your memories. And it's absolutely necessary not to let pain ruin your future." —*Lysa TerKeurst*

How about You?

Consider using these pages to write a letter to your person to begin the process of releasing regrets or offering forgiveness.

No matter how deep your sorrow, or how impossible forgiveness feels, God can be trusted to walk alongside you.

"Trust in him at all times, you people; pour out your hearts to him; for God is our refuge." Psalm 62:8, NIV

Beth Marshall

Chapter Fourteen

Did He Really Say, "You Shouldn't Feel Sad?"

Have you ever had a day where a tidal wave knocks you down before your first cup of coffee? Then, just as you regain your balance, a bigger wave slams you right back under? Yep, me too.

By the time you read this book, I hope words like "coronavirus" and "COVID-19" are ancient history, and no longer front-page news. At the time of writing this chapter, five of my closest twelve family members have tested positive for the gnarly disease our planet has been wrestling with for what seems like forever.

For the past five days, every text, call, or message was about another family who had either tested positive or who was having to quarantine at home after exposure. As I struggled to absorb the barrage of hard news, I commented to a friend that all the uncertainty and medical mayhem were making me feel really sad. His response was quick and confident, "You shouldn't feel sad." He went on to explain all the reasons I shouldn't feel sad. The symptoms could be worse, the affected kids and adults were otherwise healthy…the list went on.

Permission to Feel What You Feel

My well-intended encounter reminded me of a few things that ring true when grief, in whatever form, sneaks into your life:

- **It's okay to feel sad.** Having grown up in a wildly optimistic environment, it was okay to cry for a minute, but then your options were to get a band-aid, call an ambulance, or go outside and jump on the trampoline. Believe me when I say I'm still trying to figure out how to hold sadness and hopefulness simultaneously, but I believe both can coexist.
- **Squashing emotions can lead to unhealthy coping strategies**—mega doses of Oreos, tequila, Netflix, or whatever else feels good for a minute.
- **Comments about what you should or shouldn't feel** when you've been crushed by bad news can make you feel dismissed and shut down—that what you're feeling is not valid.

Wise Words

"It's normal to be sad when someone you love passes away. It's normal to grieve and mourn a loss. Being sad is an acceptable response to death, because really, what they would want is what I want. They'd want to be here. To be laughing. To be creating memories. Reflecting on the past, but dreaming of the future. Telling someone who is grieving not to be sad really isn't helpful. We already know our loved ones loved to see us smile. But they aren't here to see us smile, and that's sad." —Glitter and Grief

"Grief comes in waves. When a wave hits, you can't ignore it. You surf it and ride it out. My surfboard is talking to Jesus." —Pastor Rick Warren

Is It Okay to Feel Relieved?

Has there ever been someone in your life who felt like home? I'm thinking right now about my sister-in-love Kay. She felt like home to me. Kay was the one who invited me to drive her purple metallic dune buggy to high school, for seven of the most awesome hours of my entire life.

During our time at the University of Georgia, Kay and my brother Mike would let me tag along in the backseat of her VW bug on weekend trips from Athens to Atlanta. Kay never treated me like the annoying punk freshman I surely was. She treated me more like a sister.

Thirty years and lots of life later, Kay received a terrifying diagnosis consisting of two of the scariest words in the English language: "brain cancer." Nobody saw it coming. The next eighteen months were some of the hardest our family has ever known, as Kay fiercely fought this wretched beast with everything she had. Weeks after every possible kind of treatment had been exhausted, it was the day after Christmas when we got a message from my brother Mike. He suggested we come to Athens to see Kay. Several hours later, she was gone.

In the months surrounding Kay's death, endless emotions

swirled around my heart. I was grateful for the laughter, joy, and unshakable grit she brought to our family. I also felt deep sadness as we tried to imagine holidays, grandbabies, football season, and life without her. Then there was sweet relief that the hard-fought battle was no more, and that Kay was now healthier and stronger than ever, with no more tears, sadness, sickness, or sorrow.

All that to say, if someone tells you how you should or shouldn't feel, I'm sorry that happened to you. If you're experiencing sorrow, joy, devastation, relief, or anxiety… all in the same day, it's okay. Your feelings are real, and they matter.

> *However your grief turns up is valid, acceptable, and good enough."*
>
> *—Dr. Chloe*

I love the compelling words of Dr. Chloe, a psychologist who specializes in traumatic loss and grief. In her words, "However your grief turns up is valid, acceptable, and good enough."

Let It Flow

Do you ever need a minute for tears to just flow? Me too. One of the most helpful things I found for getting sadness out of my head and heart, so I can be present for the people I love most, is giving myself time and space to literally *cry it out.*

On those extra hard days when I'm missing my mom, my dad, or any of the dear ones our family has loved and lost, looking through old journals, sentimental photos, or even listening to some of their favorite music can make them feel closer. During times set apart for remembering, I give myself permission to cry, laugh, and deep dive into whatever emotions are coming to the surface.

If that sounds like your agenda for today, don't run from it. Lean in. There's healing in those tears.

Back to the Family Situation

As COVID-19 diagnoses continued pouring in, I traveled to be closer to one of our affected kids. After a day full of running around gathering groceries, medication, and anything I could imagine that might be comforting, I returned to my hotel. With no warning, the tears started to flow, and I was suddenly swept up into my first full-on tear-fest in a long time. Goodness, I needed that.

As I woke the next morning, I felt a little stronger, less overwhelmed, and ready to keep going.

How about You?

Were you ever told how you should or shouldn't feel? If so, how did you react?

Maybe you've experienced joy and sorrow, or profound pain and relief, at the same time. I encourage you to use these pages to write whatever is coming to mind.

Section Four

Reimagining the What-Ifs

Chapter Fifteen

What If Crushing Grief Doesn't Last Forever?

Have you experienced a moment when you belly laughed for the first time since loss, then wondered if something was seriously wrong with you? *How can I be riding such debilitating waves of sorrow one moment, and laughing the next? It just doesn't add up.*

In a TED Talk after losing her husband, Nora McInerny put it this way, "Grief is a multitasking emotion. You can and will be sad and happy. You will be grieving and able to love in the same year, or week—the same breath."

My dear friend Kelly is a wife, a mom, and one of the most authentic, fun, and fierce people I've ever known. I hope her story inspires you like it does me.

Kelly's Story

It was not unusual for Kelly's neighbor to pick her up after school, or for her to play all afternoon at a friend's house. So when a neighbor showed up for her in the carpool line, she didn't think anything of it. This precious nine-year-old had no idea her entire world was about to be rocked. While Kelly was at school, her beautiful, healthy, adventuresome mom, Beth Ann, suffered an extreme asthma attack, and died suddenly from complications.

Beth Ann loved people well and was generous with her time. Her happy place was being surrounded by Kelly, her brother, creativity, fun, and neighborhood friends. Her favorite things included designing custom cakes, organizing Easter egg hunts, making Kelly dresses for special occasions, and spending time with other young moms. One of Kelly's favorite jobs was helping her mom in the kitchen as she perfected her cake decorating skills. Who wouldn't love to be the icing taste tester?

> *"She was the kind of mom any kid would love to have." —Kelly Rodes*

What Friends Do

In the wake of her mom's death, Kelly fondly remembers being surrounded by loving grandparents, neighbors, and Beth Ann's dearest friends. She describes one of her mom's friends, Mrs. Sherratt, as being "kind and inclusive…calm and gentle." Without making a big deal of it, she included Kelly in whatever awesomeness was going on and made her feel like family.

Another wonderful family friend, Miss Janice, had a natural way of stepping up to make social situations less awkward. "She made me feel so normal, instead of feeling like the only girl without a mom."

Honoring Beth Ann

After Beth Ann's death, her closest friends banded together to create a fashion show fundraiser in her honor. Every year, the local Belk department store would provide the latest fashions, and Beth Ann's friends showed up to model the clothing. Proceeds from the lovely evening went to a fund designed to help kids who needed a little extra help to make college a reality.

That's what friends do.

> *"Every person needs compassion. We may not know what someone is walking through, struggling against, fighting for, or crying about in the dark hours of the night. But one thing I know—we all have tear stains on our pillow. And your unusual kindness, patience or grace may actually be the very thing God uses to reach inside their desperation and help them believe He hears their prayers." —Lysa TerKeurst*

Even now, thirty years later, the extravagant generosity Kelly and her family received from their loving community is being paid forward. Kelly, her husband, Will, and their kids, Liam and Scarlett, make a point to include neighborhood kids in their fun adventures or for a meal around the dinner table.

Growing up without a mom was nothing Kelly ever dreamed would be her story. She still misses her mom like crazy. Through the years, though, she's created a life that would surely make Beth Ann smile—a winsome home filled with lots of kids, joy, saying yes, and dreaming big dreams for the future. Kelly is living proof that life really can be beautiful again.

When Kelly and I sat down to talk about her mom, she told me, "I want to be intentional in honoring my beautiful mama. She's the first woman who taught me about mothering. She was a wonderful mama and a woman full of faith. She loved God and His people incredibly well. I am thankful she gave me a strong foundation to weather the years when she wouldn't be with me. And one day, I can't wait to stand beside her again as we worship our Lord together."

> *There will come a day when sorrow, pain, and grief aren't the loudest voices in your life.*

There will come a day when sorrow, pain, and grief aren't the loudest voices in your life.

How about You?

Have there been people, like Mrs. Sherratt, who stepped up to make your road through grief a little less difficult? If possible, you may want to let them know what a difference they made in your life.

I encourage you to write about how your loved one's personality, hobbies, or other characteristics helped shape who you are today.

Chapter Sixteen

What If You Gave Yourself Grace?
(Head Tilt, Puppy Dog Eyes)

Have you ever encountered someone with such an overwhelming I-feel-your-pain attitude, that it's actually not helpful? In fact, you might be tempted to duck down behind the spaghetti squash to avoid a conversation in the grocery store? Or maybe it's just me.

After my mom's death, casual acquaintances would sometimes approach me with sad "puppy dog eyes," and ask, with a dramatic head tilt, "So how are you doing...really?!"

While I appreciated the acknowledgement of my hard situation, I didn't always feel up to a deep-dive grief discussion in the produce aisle.

After a few of these encounters, I began to see that people really were coming from a place of care and concern and that we're all doing the best we can. I needed to figure out how to give more grace to the well-meaning people who were trying to love me.

I also realized it was okay to temporarily skip the spaghetti squash aisle if I detected sad puppy dog eyes from a distance. It was also okay to guard my heart by gently speaking up when necessary.

More Than I Could Handle

A few years ago, our son Michael went through a terrifying life-threatening illness. It was one of the hardest things our family has ever faced. Friends were so kind to text, call, or drop a note to let us know they were thinking of and praying for us. One dear friend, whose family had been through a similar situation, would regularly call to check on Michael and me. I genuinely appreciated her support and understanding. The only problem was that the calls always came right before bedtime and usually included a lot of medical questions. After receiving one of these well-intended but hard-to-handle calls, scary medical words would dance through my mind all night long.

One night when the terrifying medical terms started sneaking in, the Lord gently nudged me with this thought, "Tell those words they need to go through your Daddy (Him) before they can talk to you." I'm not kidding when I tell you it's okay to talk directly to your fears, anxieties, or whatever is harassing you—and tell them to talk to your Daddy.

I ultimately had to speak up and kindly but firmly let my well-meaning, late-calling friend know how much I appreciated her concern but that bedtime medical conversations were way more than this weary mama's heart could handle right then.

Maybe you've had to have a tough conversation with

someone trying to help, but who was actually making things a little harder.

While I'm still one hundred percent climbing the care-giving-and-receiving learning curve, it seems that gentle honesty, sprinkled with grace, will communicate what we need to say, without any hurt feelings.

Giving Yourself Grace

A messy season of mourning can make you feel as though you're doing it all wrong, and nobody understands. You may wonder if God still sees you. When self-doubt sneaks in, you might start believing some painful lies.

Why is the way we speak to ourselves often the polar opposite of how we would ever speak to a dear friend? Instead of expecting perfection, what would it be like to replace critical thoughts and words with the soothing voice of a kind, loving, understanding friend?

> *While I'm still one hundred percent climbing the care-giving-and-receiving learning curve, it seems that gentle honesty, sprinkled with grace, will communicate what we need to say, without any hurt feelings.*

One way to redirect a negative narrative sneaking in is to try and figure out where it's coming from. "Look at the return address on that." —Bob Goff

Ask yourself if the hurtful accusations you're hearing could have come from a dear friend. If not, take a moment, breathe deeply, and reframe the demoralizing message you're believing.

Instead of telling yourself…

- I don't have what it takes.
- God has forgotten about me.
- With all that brain fog, I'll surely forget about my person.
- Life will always be this hard.
- If only I had more faith, I could handle this better.

Tell yourself…

- I'm stronger than I think I am.
- God sees me. He loves me. He's with me.
- Brighter, joy-filled days are coming.
- I will get through this and remember my beloved person. There will be abundant life on the other side.
- Hey, annoying inner critic, you're not the boss of me.

When a hurtful or condemning thought tries to wiggle its way in at a traffic light—or in the spaghetti squash aisle—remind yourself, even out loud if you're feeling extra courageous, what is actually true.

"The Lord himself goes before you and will be with you; he will never leave you nor forsake you. Do not be afraid; do not be discouraged." Deuteronomy 31:8, NIV

You may want to personalize this reminder of God's ability to give you peace.

"(Your name) is not anxious about anything, but in every situation, by prayer and petition, with thanksgiving, (I am) presenting (my) requests to God. And the peace of God, which transcends all understanding, will guard (my heart) and (my mind) in Christ Jesus. (Paraphrased from Philippians 4:6-7, NIV)

How about You?

If someone, in an attempt to check in, has ever approached you with sad puppy dog eyes, or somehow missed the mark in caring for you, I encourage you (and me) to give a little extra grace.

What are some healthy, life-giving statements you could speak over yourself during these difficult days?

Use this space to write whatever is on your mind. You might also want to write your own encouraging declarations, maybe something like...

- "God is still writing my story."
- "I have lived through seriously hard things before, and I will surely make it through these times as well."

Beth Marshall

_____

_____

_____

_____

_____

_____

_____

_____

_____

_____

_____

_____

_____

_____

_____

_____

_____

_____

Chapter Seventeen

What If God Is Closer than You Think?

When your thoughts, days, and life have been hijacked by heartbreak, you may have wondered if God can, or will, heal *your* broken heart.

I get it. I mean, I'm confident that He created every single sparkling star in the sky, every zebra, gazelle, elephant, and giraffe that's ever walked the African plains, every brilliant drop of color in every rainbow that's ever been painted in the sky, and even the perfectly matched sky blue in our son's and grandson's eyes. But did I really believe He could repair the crushed pieces of my shattered heart?

Maybe you know what I'm talking about.

Attempting to spend time with the Lord in the early days of grief felt uncomfortable, even though He and I had been hanging out

> *When your thoughts, days, and life have been hijacked by heartbreak, you may have wondered if God can, or will, heal your broken heart.*

together for over ten years by that time. Most of my thoughts were more questions than anything else.

Maybe your primary question right now is *why*. Why did things have to happen the way they did? My friend, I hear you. And goodness, I wish we knew those answers. Maybe knowing why would make things a little less painful. I don't know.

But for me, why was never my primary question. The questions that would dance in my mind pretty much all day, and much of the night, were...

- *Where* do I go with all this pain?
- *When* will our kids' fun finger-painting-with-chocolate-pudding mom be back, if ever?
- *What* do I do now?

I even questioned *if* it was okay to have questions! Spoiler alert—yes, it is.

I wondered why most every time I closed my eyes to pray, I'd fall asleep. Anybody else?

My anxious mind made it not only difficult to rest at night but also incredibly hard to read, write, and especially pray.

Sometimes it felt as though there were no words to pray.

Praying When There Are No Words

In the words of Lysa TerKeurst, "I can just sit with Jesus—making no suggestions, offering no solutions. Sometimes I have nothing but quiet tears and a heavy heart. The beautiful thing is, the Bible promises when we sit with Jesus like this, the Holy Spirit lifts up the exact right prayers for me. And eventually, I sense God and there is peace...

you don't have to pray perfectly crafted prayers for the Lord to hear you or for Him to move on your behalf." —*Lysa TerKeurst*

I love that.

For a long time, my favorite parts of the Bible have been the stories of Jesus' time on earth and the healing miracles He performed. The books of Matthew, Mark, Luke, and John are filled with incredible accounts of His thirty-three years here on earth, meeting people exactly where they were. Jesus has lots of names. He is known as a Wonderful Counselor, Savior, Prince of Peace…the list goes on and on. One of His most beloved names to me is Healer.

In a society with no phones—or 24/7 global news, or texts, or Instagram, or internet—word still traveled fast when Jesus would quietly roll into a town and heal people. His healing narrative is repeated over and over through the gospels. Whether the challenge was spiritual, the inability to walk, blindness, deafness, demon possession, or disease, He did a lot of miraculous healing.

Jesus would sometimes ask a question when someone called out to Him for healing. In one well-known story a blind man called out to Jesus (Mark 10:46-52). He responded with, "What do you want me to do for you?"

"Lord, I want to see," he replied.

And Jesus healed him.

Would you ask Him to start healing your heart today?

A Turning Point

It was the one-year anniversary of losing my mom, Beazy, and I had made it almost all the way through the day with no tearful breakdowns. I was feeling confident, cool, calm, and collected. That was until I saw a group of dear friends.

Without warning, the floodgates opened, in public, surrounded by lots of people. I wish I could tell you it was Hollywood-style beautiful tears that make you actually look more lovely. Nope. This was more like out-of-control ugly crying, and I didn't know when, or if, the tears would ever stop. After a year of working feverishly to convince everyone around me that I didn't need anyone or anything, that facade vanished in an instant.

> *That night was a turning point—the moment I first believed God might be able to heal my broken heart.*

Thankfully, a friend quickly asked if he and the others could pray for me. It was crazy that even though I'd been following Jesus for over ten years, it had never occurred to me to ask anyone to pray for my deep debilitating sadness.

As several compassionate friends gathered around me, they prayed specifically that God would *take away some of the pain.* And He did.

That night was a turning point—the moment I first believed God might be able to heal my broken heart.

I wish I could tell you the sky immediately parted, my mom came back, and I was never sad again. But what did happen was a gradual shift in my heart and a realization that there actually were people who were willing to walk with me and carry some of the heavy burden of grief.

I was not alone. You, my friend, are not alone either.

A Couple Encouraging Reminders from God's Word

"Have I not commanded you? Be strong and courageous. Do not be afraid; do not be discouraged, for the Lord your God will be with you wherever you go." Joshua 1:9, NIV

"Do not be anxious about anything, but in every situation, by prayer and petition, with thanksgiving, present your requests to God. And the peace of God, which transcends all understanding, will guard your hearts and your minds in Christ Jesus." Philippians 4:6-7, NIV

How about You?

Do you believe the Lord is able to heal *your* heart? If Jesus asked you, "What do you want Me to do for you?" right now, how would you answer Him? Are you willing to let people pray for you?

Have you reached a point of admitting, "Lord, I can't do this by myself anymore"? I invite you, if you haven't already, to start praying for yourself. Is that selfish? No. It's brilliant.

> *Pray big. No more anemic, pitiful prayers, but pray believing He can do what His word promises.*

Pray big. No more anemic, pitiful prayers, but pray believing He can do what His word promises.

Lord, whatever has broken this dear one's heart, I ask with confidence for You to begin a mighty healing work.

No matter where you stand on spirituality or faith, I invite you to sit silently. Whisper Jesus' name. If you sense the Lord speaking anything to you in that moment, feel free to write about it here. God is closer than your next breath.

Section Five

Getting Uncrushed One Step at a Time

Chapter Eighteen

Sitting with Sorrow or Sprinting to a Silver Lining?

When life hurls you a monstrous curveball—like the loss of a dear person in your life—rather than trying to spin the calamity and pretend it's all good, sometimes it helps to tell it like it is.

This. Situation. Is. Hard.

Boy, that felt good.

Goodness, I wish someone had told me there's no tap dancing around grief. You can't fast-forward through it, squash it with distractions, or ignore it and pretend it has disappeared. Believe me when I say I tried! Learning to be still and feel all the emotions is one of the hardest but most important things I'm still learning.

Dear friend, we've been together for a while now, and I imagine you've figured out my natural bent is sprinting to a silver lining over sitting in sorrow. That's probably why I felt like such an amateur when grief and loss came in like a wrecking ball.

You may be wondering what healthy grief even looks like? What could you do today to be a step closer to coming out stronger on the other side?

Acknowledge the Situation

Say it out loud. Write your thoughts. Tell the Lord exactly how you're feeling. Angry? Overwhelmed? Anxious? Exhausted? Hopeless? Isolated? Tell Him. It's okay. He already knows.

Three years after Beazy's death, my dad died, and I wish someone had told me to quit trying to outrun the ache. I wish someone had whispered, "Girl, settle down. Be still. You can either find healthy ways to go through this sadness now, or it will catch up with you later."

> *"Girl, settle down. Be still. You can either find healthy ways to go through this sadness now, or it will catch up with you later."*

A Healthy Grief Habit—Clayton's Story

My friend Clayton is a wise one, and one of the kindest, most approachable humans you'll ever meet. He's a bit of an underachiever, though. Okay, not really. Clayton writes books, leads a huge ministry and summer camp, speaks all over the world, hunts bears, and honestly, could have been Billy Graham's understudy.

Several years ago, Clayton's world was rocked to the core by the deaths of both of his parents within eighteen months. As a young child, he was adopted by the most caring mom and dad a boy could ever have. Clayton respected and loved them with all his heart.

In the wake of his deep loss, this high-energy, extremely extroverted friend faced a sea of sadness unlike anything he'd ever known. He was left to figure out what the future would look like without the nurturing mom and dad who had helped shape his life.

A year or so later, I asked Clayton if there was anything in particular helping him on the pathway to healing after such great loss. He told me there actually was something. He had started a discipline of setting aside intentional daily time, maybe forty-five minutes, to get alone in a dark room, away from technology and all distractions, and do whatever his heart and body needed to do—rest, journal, be angry, cry, pray, or maybe sleep.

By prioritizing daily time to sit quietly (or not quietly) with the sorrow, instead of rushing through his grief, Clayton began to work through the hard and ever-changing emotions and began to heal.

Recognizing the Reality

Moment of confession. Sometimes it's difficult for me to let a hard reality sink deep into my soul. Whenever sudden, anticipated, or really any kind of bad news comes, my mind doesn't want to believe it. Whether it's a sad story from the other side of the globe, a tragedy down the street, or traumatic news about someone in my family, my initial instinct is to run from that new reality.

Over time, and through losing several of my closest and favorite humans, I've slowly realized the importance of getting real when tough news comes.

Stating honestly exactly what happened, even when it feels heartbreaking, can be an important first step toward healing.

- "I lost the best friend I've ever had."
- "I never got to say goodbye."
- "I'm really going to miss his quirky sense of humor, even the dad jokes."
- "The love of my life died, and I don't know how I can keep going."
- "Life without my precious child is impossible to imagine."
- "Is it normal that I don't feel any sadness at all?"
- "My friend had been sick for a long time. I didn't know I would still feel so sad."

> *Stating honestly exactly what happened, even when it feels heartbreaking, can be an important first step toward healing.*

Your Honesty Can Help Others Keep Going

Taking a look back to how you were coping when your grief was fresh and comparing it to where you are now can help you see where healing has already taken place. You can also be a lifeline to somebody else who's struggling to see any glimmers of light cracking through the dark.

I love this message on a popular Facebook grief support group page:

"Today marks 11 years since my brother passed away from a sudden cardiac death at 17 years of age. As I reflect on the day and remember him, I think back to the events and emotions of day one.

The feelings I felt were unimaginable and left me and my family devastated and utterly destroyed with grief. It was nearly impossible to tackle every minute, let alone imagine my remaining years without my brother.

Here I am though.

Today we remembered him in our own ways, and yes it hurts deeply. The loss is always there.

But today I was also able to:

- log on and do some work
- enjoy a coffee with my family
- play with my niece
- be grateful for today and for life
- reflect on my time with my brother, remember the laughs, fun and the memories together

What I am trying to say is that *it's insane how time can change the severity of your grief and allow you to live life once again. Live without feeling guilty each day, without feeling physically sick. Feeling okay to have a laugh, smile, and feel excited for something on the horizon.*

Of course I have bad days, sometimes horrible days. It's not been easy.

I just hope this gives a bit of hope for anyone who feels so heavily weighed down by grief today, especially around this time of year and also if you're in the early days." —Jacinta Wilson

Here are a couple of the many responses Jacinta received:

"This is the most helpful post I've read so far. Thank you so much for sharing."

"Thank you for this, Jacinta. This is the kind of support I need the most in my grief—hope of happiness and future. I'm so happy you wrote this!"

How about You?

If you've ever felt stuck in sorrow, this exercise is an excellent starting point for recognizing the reality of what you're going through. Get it out of your heart and head and onto paper.

Today, are you feeling stable, put together, perfectly hydrated, rested, and like you just ran ten miles? Awesome. Seriously, that is wonderful news, if that describes you.

Or maybe you're experiencing anger, frustration, joylessness, anxiety, heartache, confusion, disappointment with God, or something else difficult. That's okay too.

Maybe your days are a bit of a mixed bag, like Jacinta described above. That's perfectly fine as well.

Would you consider trying Clayton's tip of setting aside some daily time to do the hard work of grieving? Here's space to write about whatever you're thinking or feeling—anything you want to get off your chest and onto paper. No judgment. I promise.

"Blessed are those who mourn, for they will be comforted."
Matthew 5:4, NIV

Beth Marshall

_____

_____

_____

_____

_____

_____

_____

_____

_____

_____

_____

_____

_____

_____

_____

_____

_____

_____

_____

_____

Chapter Nineteen

"So How's Your Mom?" and
Other Grief Triggers

I t was a wonderfully tear-free day when sweet Martha, the dress shop owner downtown, innocently asked, "So how's your mom, Beth?"

It took everything in me to suck up the tears and explain. "Oh, I guess you haven't heard. She passed away a couple weeks ago."

It was impossible for me to imagine anyone's life carrying on like normal, when mine had come to a screeching halt.

Grief triggers can take the wind out of your sails. For you, maybe it's a whiff of fresh gingerbread that takes you right back to your grandmom's house at Christmas, but now, instead of feeling joyful, you're holding back tears. Or maybe it was a letter arriving in

> *It was impossible for me to imagine anyone's life carrying on like normal, when mine had come to a screeching halt.*

your mailbox, addressed to your deceased loved one, that took your breath away.

What Is a Grief Trigger?

Grief triggers are—often unexpected—reminders that wash over you like a tidal wave. Sometimes, just when you've gotten back on your feet, a violent wave crashes you back under with no warning.

These sneaky moments, also known as "grief bursts" or "grief bombs," can be tied to sights—maybe a granddad playing at the park with his grandkids will remind you that your kids' granddad is gone. Or a sound might escort you right back to happier, more carefree times. My mom's favorite song, "59th Street Bridge Song," aka "Feeling Groovy," by Simon & Garfunkel still gets me every single time.

It could be a fragrance or a holiday that knocks you right back under a tumultuous wave of sorrow.

Events can be difficult triggers, particularly unavoidable things like a father/daughter or mother/son dance, a baby shower, a wedding, Grandparents' Day, "Muffins with Mom" or "Doughnuts with Dad" days at school, Bring Your Child to Work Day…the list is endless. Putting the potentially triggering events on the calendar can be a helpful way to preemptively guard your heart.

Triggers happen around important anniversaries, other special days, or on an ordinary Tuesday in the carpool line. That's what makes them so insidious—you rarely see them coming. Attending any funeral can quickly bring back memories of your loved one's memorial service.

A Few Tips for Managing Triggers

- **Don't fight it.** Go with it. Lean into it. Cry if you need to cry. Laugh if you need to laugh.
- **Breathe deeply** for three minutes in this rhythm— four seconds in, through your nose, six seconds out, through your mouth. It seems so simple but can actually slow your mind down and give you a sense of calm.
- **Let someone know when a difficult day is coming,** so you won't be caught off guard and feel so alone.
- **Designate a safe place to be alone, if you need it.** Your car, an outside space, even a closet can provide a quiet place and alone time when a trigger hits.
- **If gatherings are hard for you right now, there's no shame in opting out**—or you might consider leaving a getaway car parked somewhere you can easily escape to, if crowds or specific events make you panic.

The Allergy Doctor Trigger, Twenty-One Years Later

The evening of my mom's sudden death, her beloved husband, Herb, tried frantically to contact family members to get the name of her allergist. Beazy was highly allergic to wasps, hornets, yellow jackets, and most any kind of flying creature. Every time she got stung, the reaction was quicker and more extreme, to the point of her instantly passing out, and a subsequent trip to the emergency room. We have always wondered if some kind of a sting led to her sudden cardiac arrest.

Last week, I never saw the grief bomb coming. I was at my regular annual allergist visit, discussing my (also extreme) bee allergies with the doctor. As the appointment wrapped, she told me I seemed to be doing great after several years of allergy shots and suggested I might want to go on a maintenance level of treatment. My wise allergist must have seen the expression on my face change to panic. She suddenly asked if I was fearful of getting stung.

Her innocent question triggered me like nobody's business, as warm tears began to stream down my face. I wasn't trying to be dramatic but shared a bit of my mom's story so the doctor would understand my unexpected tearful reaction. I immediately told her I was sorry for crying, as though the tears were intentional.

If you've ever apologized for feeling sadness, you get it.

My compassionate doctor handed me a tissue, as she fought back her own tears. Maybe my reaction reminded her how much she loves her own mom? I don't know. What I know is that I never expected to be triggered in such a visible way, twenty-one years after losing my mom.

Whether the person you're missing died two weeks, two years, or two decades ago, grief triggers don't mean you're weak or that you haven't made any progress.

These sudden waves of emotion are a reflection of how deeply your loved one impacted your life and are nothing to be ashamed of.

"Trust in him at all times, you people; pour out your hearts to him, for God is our refuge." Psalm 62:8, NIV

No matter how deep your sorrow, God can be trusted to bring peace and healing.

How about You?

Every one of us grieves differently. Triggers may not affect you much at all. Or these unexpected bursts of emotion might suffocate you.

These sudden waves of emotion are a reflection of how deeply your loved one impacted your life and are nothing to be ashamed of.

Either way, it's okay to feel however you feel—sad, not sad, devastated, exhausted, embarrassed, weak, angry, stuck. It's all okay. Instead of pretending you've got it all together when your world has actually fallen apart, writing about it can help.

Have you experienced a grief trigger? If so, how did it make you feel?

Are there any ways you could prepare ahead of time for a potentially triggering event or a "So how's your mom (or whoever you are missing)?" kind of question? Here's space to write about whatever's coming to mind about grief triggers.

Chapter Twenty

Secret Weapons for Getting Unstuck

Have you ever gotten so caught up in mourning, you weren't sure you'd ever find your way out? I surely have.

At the time of Beazy's death, I was in year twenty of my twenty-five year career with Delta Air Lines. My favorite part of the Delta adventure was flying international trips, especially to Munich, Germany. Interacting with a jumbo jet full of strangers and working alongside different flight attendants and pilots every week were sweet distractions from the sorrow. Work was an easy place to hide.

It was much less stressful to make small talk at Oktoberfest in my broken German than to have a heart-to-heart conversation with someone who knew me in real life.

Much more difficult than going to work were the days spent at home alone with my thoughts.

> *It was much less stressful to make small talk at Oktoberfest in my broken German than to have a heart-to-heart conversation with someone who knew me in real life.*

Home is where the intense reality of grief got my full attention. On a typical day after the kids had gone to school, I'd put on my hideous navy blue sweats, my "grief uniform," and curl up in a cozy chair. That's where I'd attempt to spend time with the Lord and write in my spiral prayer journal. Truth be told, many of those hours were more crying than actually reading, writing, or praying.

One morning, I remember feeling a nudge from the Lord to write about my mom. Write about her? Really? *How cool,* I thought. *I'd love to, but my mind is so foggy right now. Lord, You're going to have to help me remember things.*

I started to write. The Lord gently brought recent and long-ago memories to my mind faster than I could put them down. For two solid hours, hardly moving a muscle, I scribbled life stories on the tear-stained pages of my prayer journal. I wrote about evenings spent playing our black upright piano and singing loudly. Mom was clearly my most loyal musical fan, as she'd repeatedly request her favorite Broadway tunes. Don't get me wrong, Mom is the only person who ever requested an encore, but her enthusiasm always kept the music flowing. Apparently, the volume made up for lack of musical perfection.

I wrote about the day she called me in my dorm at the University of Georgia, ecstatic that she'd invited the entire Emory University Dental Fraternity to our house for Thanksgiving dinner.

We had a dental student friend from California who was not able to go home for Thanksgiving, so why not invite him and all of his handsome soon-to-be-dentist friends to share the holiday? I have no idea what the turkey tasted like that year, but I do remember it being the most wonderful Thanksgiving!

Beazy is also the one who, when a grandchild accidentally spilled a two-liter beverage on her (formerly) off-white carpet, would quickly grab paper towels, clean up the disaster, and add her signature phrase, "No problem with Beazy." It was ridiculously hard to get on her last nerve. But goodness, I know her kids and grands must have come dangerously close!

In my journal, I wrote every sweet, embarrassing, serious, and hilarious memory I could recall. As decades of stories filled the pages, I began to smile and even laugh through the tears. Thanks to the Lord's whisper to write through the sorrow, my tears of sadness slowly became tears of thankfulness for the rare and extraordinary woman we called Beazy.

"Finally, brothers and sisters, whatever is true, whatever is noble, whatever is right, whatever is pure, whatever is lovely, whatever is admirable—if anything is excellent or praiseworthy—think about such things." Philippians 4:8, NIV

Writing the real stuff with honesty, tears, and even humor can help you feel close to your person.

A Few Prompts You Might Want to Think and Write About

- What do you want people to know about your loved one? Their kindness, hobbies, intellect, sense of humor, athletic skills, generosity? What else?
- Today, what I'm missing most is…
- Five words that describe you best are…
- My favorite things we used to do together were…

- The part of you I hope forever lives on through me is...
- A conversation I wish we could have had would have been about...

> *Writing the real stuff with honesty, tears, and even humor can help you feel close to your person.*

Freewriting

Here are a few tips for writing without prompts: Don't over-think it. Just start writing. Words, phrases, life-changing or ordinary experiences. Goodness, not-so-goodness, words, notes, phrases, sentences—whatever comes to mind when you think about them. No worries if you run out of things to write about. You can always come back in a few days, weeks, months, or anytime you want to keep writing their story.

Favorite Day

Is there a favorite day or a season you hope to never forget? Think about...

- a long-ago story you might have forgotten
- a time that made you laugh out loud
- an exceptional vacation
- an event, concert, play, music, restaurant, or whatever it was you enjoyed together

Print Photos

Instead of saving all your photos exclusively on your phone or computer, print some of the most special ones and add them to your journal or right here on the pages of *Uncrushed*. What a glorious keepsake you'll be creating!

How about You?

Do you have a special place to preserve stories? If you're experiencing grief-related brain fog, you are not alone. Stories may be difficult to remember right now. If so, you might want to ask the Lord to bring things to mind. Ask Him what *He* loved about your person.

In a separate journal, a spiral notebook, or right here, I encourage you, if you haven't already, to start writing. You don't have to do it all today. It's not homework. Take your time. This sacred practice of remembering can be a huge turning point in your healing.

*Special note to the person whose grief is complicated, confusing, or may be slowly unfolding over many years. I never intend to minimize what you have been through. Your journey is your journey, and some of the emotions you're experiencing might be triggering, or better expressed with a professional therapist or pastor.

Beth Marshall

Chapter Twenty-One

Embracing Both Joy and Sorrow

The Day That Changed Everything

My friend Mandy Smith is one of the fiercest and most fun people I know. The Lord brought us together ten years ago, in the final days of her beloved husband, Zac's courageous battle with cancer. Zac was thirty-three years old when he died.

Mandy and their kids have always had a unique ability to embrace joy and sorrow, even in the midst of unthinkably hard days. Thankfully Zac was able to be at home along with Mandy and his parents, as hospice angels cared for their family. Mandy and I devised a plan for me to pick up their three young children during Zac's final hours. Even though Luke, Jake, Lizzy, and I barely knew each other, the Lord gave us the most marvelous moments together, even on the day that would change their lives forever.

The kids buckled up in my car, as threatening dark clouds surrounded us. Mandy casually mentioned, "Oh yeah, the kids are terrified of storms." *Awesome,* I thought. As we pulled out of the driveway, torrential quarter-sized hail began to plummet my car. All three kids started to laugh hysterically. They thought the hail was amazing and so cool. Only God could have orchestrated their reactions and protected their tender hearts for what was to come.

Later, at our house, we somehow ended up lighting fire-crackers and finger painting with chocolate pudding on the kitchen counter. Thanks, Lizzy, for telling your mom, "Miss Beth let us light matches." Oops. The photos of Mandy's kids covered in chocolate pudding, on the same day their world was being forever rocked, became priceless reminders of God's goodness, even in the darkest storms.

As the kids continued playing, Mandy called with the news that Zac's enduring battle was over. I'll never forget her one request that day. She asked if the kids could stay a little longer.

"Of course," I responded. Mandy added, "Once I tell them this news, their lives will never be the same again." She was so right.

Saving the Good Stuff

In the difficult months to come, Mandy wanted to be sure she did everything possible to hold Zac's legacy close. Some of the wonderful ideas she implemented, besides preserving the chocolate pudding–covered face photos, were...

- having a soft quilt created for each child from some of their dad's favorite shirts
- hanging onto Denver Broncos memorabilia Zac and the kids had shared together
- giving Luke, Jake, and Lizzy each a grief journal for writing and drawing pictures

- saving photos from the day they met Tim Tebow in Denver, as their dad was honored at a Broncos game

> *Through it all, she refuses to let her crushing life circumstances crush her joy.*

Mandy has shown me over and over what faith, hope, love, and perseverance can look like since she became a way-too-young widow and a single mom.

Through it all, she refuses to let her crushing life circumstances crush her joy.

Some Other Way-Too-Young Widows

One of the greatest joys in my ministry to grieving people has been spending time with the phenomenal women of the American Widow Project (AWP). This extraordinary organization provides support for some of America's finest and bravest: US military widows.

Every year, the AWP hosts long weekend events for some of these courageous survivors. Along with a couple AWP leading ladies, the guests gather in a huge home, in various spectacular locations around the country. These special getaways are a rare opportunity for the military widows (Gold Star Wives) to rest, refresh, laugh, cry, share their heroes' stories, go on adventures, and find support from people who understand their unique journey.

Before going to speak at a weekend getaway in Phoenix, Arizona, I asked Mandy (see story above) if she had any insight or wise words to share with the "widow sisters" who would be attending. Here's a bit of a letter I shared with the AWP sisters, including some of Mandy's creative and funny tips she put together for them.

Dear AWP friends,

Your beautiful photos and compelling stories have profoundly touched my heart and undoubtedly the heart of America. While I've never walked in your shoes, I have had the honor to walk alongside my dear friend Mandy and her three kids this year since the crushing death of her beloved husband, and their dad, Zac. He was thirty-three years old.

Mandy has allowed me a front row seat to her life as a young widow. Like her, you may not be comfortable asking for a lot of help. I get it. That's why I want to share a few of her compelling thoughts she wrote recently to thank some of the people who've shown up for her family with creativity, compassion, and love.

My hope is that you, too, will be showered by unexpected acts of awesomeness by your community. You deserve all the very best.

Love, Beth

Here is Mandy's letter:

"Dear friends and family, I love it when:

- **you help without asking,** like the church home group who moved us into our home.
- **you take my kids places.** When you love on my kids, you're loving on me and on Zac—all at the same time.
- **you do things I can't possibly do,** like mowing my

forest lawn. One friend just comes and does that for me.

- **you help me with computer stuff.** Zac was the computer guy, not me.
- **you take the kids shopping for times like Christmas and Mother's Day**...not so much that I need gifts, so much as it's important for them to be able to give.

I'll never get over when:

- **old friends call or email the kids.** Sometimes they'll tell a funny story about their dad. I love that. I talk about Zac all the time, but when a cool guy who was a friend of their dad's has something to say, it's the best story ever.
- **you created handmade quilts** from some of Zac's things, for me and each of the kids."

And here is Mandy's honest and slightly hilarious partial list of things not to say or do. I bet you can relate.

"Don't give me sad eyes when you see me. I'm not a stray puppy. Don't tell me, 'He's in a better place.' I know that, but really the best place I can think of for him to be right now is in the bedroom waiting for me. Or doing laundry. :) Love, Mandy"

I love how Mandy and the kids honor Zac by continuing to tell his story and being a giant blessing to others.

How about You?

How has your community, church, or friend group been there

for you? Are there ways you wish people could make your life a little easier? Recording ways people have been there for you is a great reminder that you're not alone.

Here's space to write about how you have or haven't felt cared for through your mourning. Also, if you sometimes feel joy and sorrow simultaneously, you may want to write about that experience as well. What practical ways have you come up with to keep memories fresh?

Beth Marshall

_____

_____

_____

_____

_____

_____

_____

_____

_____

_____

_____

_____

_____

_____

_____

_____

_____

Uncrushed

Chapter Twenty-Two

Love, Loss, and Extravagant Generosity...a Living Legacy

T he thought of navigating the first Thanksgiving without Zac was overwhelming for Mandy's family. That's why Mandy, Lizzy, Jake, and Luke (chapter twenty-one) put their heads together to figure out how to make the most of this ridiculously hard day. They decided to reach out to a local family who had been living for thirty years with a chronic medical situation and deliver a magnificent Thanksgiving feast. Mandy, along with the kids, shopped for the food and then cut, diced, baked, carved, and created the loveliest Thanksgiving masterpiece. The recipient family could not believe the amazing kindness from this newly-bereaved mom and kids, just six months after their own profound loss.

That's how the Smith family's journey of beginning to heal, through giving back, started.

Over the years, their tradition evolved into an annual "Friendsgiving" feast, where anyone without a place to go for Thanksgiving was welcome. There was always room for one more around their ever-expanding table. Zac's legacy state-ment on the wall of their home is a timeless reminder to all who visit, that "God is still God & God is still good. To God be the glory."

Shortly after Zac's death, Mandy and the kids wanted to express their appreciation to the medical staff at the cancer clinic who had taken extraordinary care of Zac. They initiated an annu-al Doughnut Day. Every year on Zac's birthday, they'd shower the compassionate staff with dozens of fresh doughnuts. This thoughtful tradition continued for years until they recently moved back to Arizona to be closer to family.

> *"God is still God & God is still good. To God be the glory."*
> *—Zac Smith*

Mandy's family's extravagant generosity has been a secret weapon—not only to soften the heartbreak of grief but also to turn their painful mess into a mighty message of kindness and thankfulness.

How about You?

Mandy and her kids have taught me volumes about the val-ue of showing gratitude on their journey of life since Zac's death. Please use this space to write whatever thoughts are coming to mind. Is there someone who has made a difference on your path toward healing? Sending a quick note of thanks can brighten not only your day but also their day when that note arrives.

Uncrushed

_____

_____

_____

_____

_____

_____

_____

_____

_____

_____

_____

_____

_____

_____

_____

_____

_____

_____

_____

_____

Section Six

Keep Going, My Friend

Chapter Twenty-Three

Holiday Survival Kit

The music, yummy aromas, and shimmering lights all conjure up memories of the most wonderful time of the year. But when you're missing someone you love, the holidays can magnify the deep loss you're feeling.

When my family lost a couple of our closest and favorite people—different years, but both within weeks of the holidays—"merry and bright" seemed a thousand miles in the rearview mirror. Maybe you understand what I'm talking about.

I remember how impossible it felt to quickly pivot to joy and imagine what Thanksgiving and Christmas might look like in this new context. Do you carry on as though nothing is different, even though there's a crater-sized hole in your heart and a painfully empty chair at the table?

And what about the kids? Should you continue some of the family traditions for their sake, even when it feels weird and sad?

At the times of Beazy's and Kay's deaths, a root canal

sounded more appealing than hours of small talk and cocktail weenies at the annual Christmas parties. Did I still have to go?

If decorating, parties, house guests, shopping, and holiday cooking spark joy for you, by all means, go for it. But, if the thought of adding one thing to your life right now is making you hyperventilate, give yourself permission to stop the insanity and bring it all down a notch.

Keep It Simple

Can you imagine November and December without a manic pace of endless events? It might take a little rethinking about what you've always done, but being intentional to schedule lots of evenings at home with your closest people is a wonderful way to be kind to yourself. Taking control of your holiday calendar can create a sense of calm, even during a chaotic season.

> *If decorating, parties, house guests, shopping, and holiday cooking spark joy for you, by all means, go for it. But, if the thought of adding one thing to your life right now is making you hyperventilate, give yourself permission to stop the insanity and bring it all down a notch.*

Here are a few practical tips for surviving the holidays while grieving. I hope they help.

- Make a plan with those closest to you so the holiday doesn't sneak up on you.
- You have nothing to prove. Do whatever holiday

decorating you love or no decorating, if that suits you better.

- Consider a change of menu or a change of venue.
- Take time every day to rest.
- Include the kids in pre-holiday planning. If there is a tradition that's important to them, try to include it, if it isn't too exhausting for you.
- Consider drawing names for family gifts, rather than running yourself ragged to purchase a gift for every single person.
- Make a memory. Ice skating, making pottery together, going to a play or concert, instead of buying lots of gifts, can be a fun way to bring a little holiday cheer.
- Spend a quiet day at home, go on a cruise, or somehow get away 'til the season is over. If that's your healthiest option this year, it's your healthiest option. Let your closest people know, honestly, what you can and can't handle around the holidays.

This holiday season, spend more time with people and doing things that energize you and less time with those people and things that ~~suck the living daylights out of~~ exhaust you.

Keep It Fresh

Set aside some time to tell and retell favorite stories about the person you're missing. Say their name, and give others permission to do the same.

One of my favorite memories of my hilarious sister-in-law Kay was the year she led a girls' trip to New York City.

For several days, it was all Hard Rock Cafe, Broadway musicals, Carmine's Italian Restaurant, and full-contact shopping. Good thing no brothers or husbands were included on Kay's invite list. Shopping with those guys in the city would have been like fishing with the game warden. :)

> *Set aside some time to tell and retell favorite stories about the person you're missing. Say their name, and give others permission to do the same.*

Write Them a Letter

From time to time, I still love to write a letter to the people I'm missing, mostly to say thanks for the difference they made in my life. Here's an example of one I wrote to my mom a few years ago.

Dear Mom,

It's Christmas week, and goodness, I miss you. You would ADORE your eleven precious grand- and twenty-two great-grandpeople! They are fun and wild passionate individuals, just like we were. There are a few things I hope I'll never forget about you:

-the smocked Christmas dresses, and ~~smocked jumpsuits~~ super-hero outfits you made for the little boys.

-the year eight-year-old Amy decorated her bedroom for you, with 100% red lights. You were so thoughtful to not tell her it looked like Bourbon Street in New Orleans.

-the first New Year's Day in my new job with Delta Air Lines.

I loved it when you showed up at the ATL airport with our family's German tradition—sauerkraut and pork, on a pie plate. Who knew that re-cooked sauerkraut, cooked on full blast in the First Class oven, could nearly cause a Boeing 727 evacuation?

Mom, thanks for making the holidays crazy fun and for loving all five of your kids the most.

I will always love you, Beth

How about You?

If you're missing someone you love this Christmas, I encourage you to use these pages to write any thoughts you have around navigating this first, second, or any subsequent holiday season. Include ways you might change things up or adjust the agenda for this year. Is there a familiar tradition you want to be sure and keep or a new one you'd like to start?

Consider setting aside some time to write a letter to your person, if you're feeling up to it.

_____

_____

_____

_____

_____

_____

_____

_____

_____

_____

_____

_____

_____

_____

_____

_____

_____

_____

_____

_____

_____

Beth Marshall

_____

_____

_____

_____

_____

_____

_____

_____

_____

_____

_____

_____

_____

_____

_____

_____

Chapter Twenty-Four

The Year-Round Holidays
Are Not the Boss of You

D o you ever say yes to things that don't spark any joy? If you're tired of attempting to keep an impossible schedule around any holiday, this could be the year to stop the insanity. Whether it's New Year's Day, Mother's Day, Father's Day or another holiday, recognizing that YOU are the boss of your schedule can help.

Often the anticipation leading up to a holiday is more anxiety producing than the actual day. Additionally, you may experience deeper emotions the second year after the death, as reality deeply sets in.

Here are a few tips for taking back your holiday, no matter what time of year it is.

Father's Day

If this will be your first Father's Day since losing your dad, a beloved child, or another important male in your life, let someone trusted know if you're feeling apprehensive. Call someone who has experienced a similar loss, and tell them exactly how you're feeling.

Deciding ahead of time how you plan to spend the day can help you feel a little more in control when the actual holiday arrives.

"Father's Day is usually an emotional struggle for me—and this year the weight is even greater because I'm still grieving the loss of my dad last December. Grief is an unexpected emotion which seems to come in waves triggered by special days, smiles, places, hobbies, sounds, songs, really… just life.

I try to experience and digest it as it comes instead of stuffing it down because…it's not healthy." —Sharie King

Mother's Day

Whether you're missing your mom, grandmom, aunt, precious child, or someone else this Mother's Day—it's impossible to escape the 24/7 flow of images of happy families celebrating together. You may be wondering how you'll get through not just the day, but an entire season leading up to a day that's all about moms and kids.

Nana

On Mother's Day, I always reminisce about not only my mom, Beazy, but also our one-in-a-million grandmom, Nana.

Surely with no sadness, tears, carb-counting, or keto craziness in Heaven, Nana's world-class six-layer chocolate cake

> *Surely with no sadness, tears, carb-counting, or keto craziness in Heaven, Nana's world-class six-layer chocolate cake will be on the guilt-free heavenly menu every day, right?*

will be on the guilt-free heavenly menu every day, right?

Reply All

Another favorite family tradition for keeping memories fresh is to stir up an email conversation on special days like Mother's Day.

Here's how it works. My cousin Drew might start the day with an email to all the cousins, with a humorous reminder about Nana's *Steel Magnolia*–ish approach for getting home improvement projects accomplished.

"While you're on your feet…could you possibly clean out the gutters and paint the guest room?" —Nana

Another family member might "reply all" with the classic memory of Nana's glory days, serving as a private duty nurse for baseball legend Ty Cobb. I guarantee you his room was tidy, with no cobwebs, while Nana was his ~~boss~~ nurse.

Later in the day, another of Nana's grandkids might share a familiar memory of spending a solo night at her cozy cottage home. At Nana's house, you could stay up late to watch the Atlanta Braves, then sleep in crispy pink sheets. What's not to love about that?

> *Reply-all stories can momentarily shift your focus from the sadness of your person's death to the goodness and uniqueness of their life.*

Reply-all stories can momentarily shift your focus from the sadness of your person's death to the goodness and uniqueness of their life.

Grief Cannot Win

"Mother's Day has been tricky for me since Tate (three months old) died. I will never look at pictures of my kids without noticing the two that are missing. (More of Tate and Brinkley's stories in chapter thirty-two.) I was anxious about Mother's Day this year without being able to see my mom. I miss her every day, so not sure why I thought that day would be any different.

*I've gotten to the point over the years that I've decided **grief cannot win**. It cannot have my marriage, my children or my Mother's Day.*

So on Sunday, I was thankful for the 35 years I had with my mom. I have so many incredible memories…and I was thankful for the perspective this life's journey has given me." —Whitney Kirby

How about You?

If there's a holiday on the horizon, have you considered how you plan to spend it? A few thoughts about holidays:

- Lean into whatever you're feeling. Cry when you need to. Laugh when you need to.
- Buy yourself a gift they would have given you.

- Make or purchase a delicious meal or six-layer chocolate cake, or whatever reminds you of them.
- Spend the day somewhere that soothes your soul.
- Be kind to yourself.
- Do whatever you're feeling up to. If spending a quiet day at home is what you're feeling up to…do it.
- Make a plan, but know it's okay to scrap the whole deal if it's too much to handle.
- Take a nap.

Are any ideas coming to mind for acknowledging an upcoming special day? Would the "reply-all" email chain be something your family and friends might want to try? I invite you to use these pages to reflect and write your thoughts around coping with holidays and other important days.

_____

_____

_____

_____

_____

_____

_____

_____

_____

_____

_____

_____

_____

_____

_____

_____

_____

_____

_____

Beth Marshall

_____

_____

_____

_____

_____

_____

_____

_____

_____

_____

_____

_____

_____

_____

_____

_____

Chapter Twenty-Five

Tears in My Spinach Omelet

There's no time limit on grief. It takes as long as it takes.

It was Mother's Day weekend, and our grown kids were scattered across the country. The kind invitation from our daughter Amy to come visit her in the Colorado Rocky Mountains sounded like perfection. Before my early morning flight, I stopped at an airport cafe for breakfast. My eighteen-year-old server welcomed me with a warm smile. It was obvious he was excellent at his job, a natural people person.

As Lamar delivered my coffee and spinach omelet, we struck up a conversation about Mother's Day. The friendly teenager's face lit up as he talked about his beautiful mom. They loved spending time together. Lamar referred to himself unashamedly as a "mama's boy." She had to be so proud of her kind and delightful son.

As I finished my breakfast, Lamar returned to check on me and politely asked me about my

> *There's no time limit on grief. It takes as long as it takes.*

mom. I casually responded, "She is in Heaven." There was no way to predict how my face would turn red, and spawn gigantic tears welling up in my eyes, from those four simple words.

It had been fifteen years since my mom's sudden graduation to Heaven. Maybe that's why the ambush of anxiety took me so off guard.

I could feel the ache in Lamar's heart, thinking he had upset me. But my own heart melted as my new eighteen-year-old counselor sat down next to me and gently patted my back, assuring me it was okay to cry.

I didn't have the heart to tell Lamar, through the mascara dripping down my cheeks, that I spend much of my life speaking and writing to help *other people* find hope after loss. Nor did I have the guts to tell him his words, "It's okay to cry," are quoted almost verbatim in my *Grief Survivor* book. I doubt he would have believed me anyway.

Lamar's compassion and kind words reminded me of an important truth. It really is okay to cry, and it's okay to laugh—no matter how long it's been.

If you're missing your mom, child, dad, sister, brother, or anyone else right now, I pray the Lord will place an angel like Lamar on your path, right when you need him most.

> *The goal of grieving is not to "get over" your person but to celebrate your loved one's life and find ways to keep them close to your heart.*

The goal of grieving is not to "get over" your person but to celebrate your loved one's life and find ways to keep them close to your heart.

"If you have a friend going through something tough, instead of asking, 'Are you OK?', text this: 'You are strong and brave. And if you ever have a day you forget that, I'm here to remind you.'"—Lysa TerKeurst

Catching a Grief Bomb Before It Lands

Sometimes you can see it coming—a potentially painful event. What if you could defuse an incoming grief bomb before it lands?

When you've recently experienced a miscarriage or the loss of a beloved child, a baby shower might be too much for you to handle right now. Or maybe it's a wedding or bridal shower that's making anxiety rise up in your heart.

> *If you need to opt out of an upcoming event, give yourself permission to do whatever you need to do to take care of you.*

Attending another funeral can be a massive trigger when you're still reeling from your own front row seat at a lost loved one's service.

If you need to opt out of an upcoming event, give yourself permission to do whatever you need to do to take care of you.

There are plenty of ways to acknowledge a marriage, a friend's baby on the way, or a death in someone else's family without attending in-person. Sending a thoughtful note, or a gift, when appropriate, might be your better option than showing up, if a particular event is hitting too close to home.

There's No Shame in Canceling

Even if you RSVP'd yes, then realize you're not up to being around a lot of people, give yourself permission to cancel your plans. There's no need to come up with a ~~flaky~~ creative excuse—I'm sick, I need to rewire the Wi-Fi, the dog needs a bath—it's okay to tell the truth. "Grief is really hard for me right now. I'm sorry I can't be there."

Are you comfortable canceling plans for a situation that's potentially triggering? There's no need for a lengthy explanation. "I'm sorry, but I won't be able to make it" is good enough.

> *"Closure is for bank accounts, not love accounts." —Dr. Alan Wolfelt*

How about You?

Are you comfortable shedding a tear for someone, even if it's been a long time? Is there an event coming up that you might need to reconsider before responding to the invite?

What is something you've discovered since your loss? If you've ever had a "tears in your spinach omelet" moment, write about that too.

You are stronger than you think you are. Choosing your activities carefully is an important part of taking care of you.

Section Seven

Good Grief

Chapter Twenty-Six

Grief Friends

Have you ever had a friend who asks how you're doing, and you automatically respond "fine," but they know you're not? So they dig a little deeper? If so, this chapter's for you.

People don't always show up the way we thought they would after a traumatic loss. Chances are, they might be afraid of saying something hurtful and making things worse for you. Or maybe their own grief is still so fresh and raw, they don't feel like they'd be much help.

Sometimes a "grief friend" comes along at just the right moment. When is the right moment? Any time you're feeling alone, overwhelmed, crushed, or confused after loss.

A grief friend may have experienced a similar loss to what you're going through. Their unique understanding

Grief friend:/grēf frend/

a special person who may not have been in your inner circle of friends, but who shows up for you anyway.

and presence can bring unexpected support and much-needed companionship. Sometimes, this friend will become a forever friend.

"There is a gentle ease that comes with knowing grief and being around others who know grief too. It's a connection that creates a common language, but also allows for understanding the unspoken. It's a connection that makes explaining unnecessary." —Alex Mammadyarov

What Does a Grief Friend Do?

They show up, and keep showing up even when the dust settles. They record important dates, so they can be there for you months, even years, down the road. Lots of people jump in with support at the beginning, but a grief friend might take it a step further and...

- call you in the evening, if they know that's your hardest time of day. When you tell her you're in your pajamas, she offers to come over in her pjs too, if you're needing a little company.
- stop by with your favorite snack on a dark winter day
- curate an album of your meaningful photos for you
- bring dinner by your house and offer to stay and dine with you, if you're feeling alone
- send a care package with bath salts, a candle, dark chocolate, or anything that might be comforting for you

Tamsin Millard, host of the *Not So Linear* podcast, is

grateful for the grief friends she's come to know through Motherless Daughters in Sydney, Australia. In her words:

"Grief can be lonely, but it doesn't have to be. There's nothing better than connecting with someone who just gets you, who knows how you feel. Not just the pain of losing a mum and growing up without her, but also the absence of her in our future."

"We talk about our mums, laugh, joke, and provide comfort for each other in a way other people can't. We just get it."

"When you find your community everything feels easier." —*Tamsin Millard*

What Really Mattered through Grief

I posted a question for my Facebook friends asking what mattered most to them during their toughest times of loss. Here are a few of their responses:

My dear sister-in-love Anna shared that "a friend drove three hours to sit with me and pray when my daddy died. How strengthening and powerful it was."

Wanda told me it meant the world "when friends and family shared memories of my mother-in-law. We would sit, laugh, cry, and share all the stories that made her happy. I could see she was loved and cherished by so many."

Anna S. said it meant the world to "have lunch with some of my mom's oldest friends, and hear their stories about her from long ago, before I came along."

Taco Soup and Quilts

A couple weeks after losing my dear sister-in-love Kay, I got a call from my friend Leslie. She will never drop the "call if you need anything" bomb on you during a traumatic time, when you have no idea what you need. No, she shows up. Leslie brings something yummy, hugs you around the neck, and lets you know that you don't have to conquer this giant by yourself.

Practically speaking, she'll call to let you know the taco soup is on the stove and will be delivered to your back door in twenty minutes, tomorrow night, or whenever it's convenient for you. Over the years, I've realized that it's really not just about the taco soup. It's also about acknowledging the crushing losses and also showing up to celebrate all the goodness—like the birth of a precious grandbaby.

A few years ago, Leslie appeared at the back door with two of the most breathtakingly beautiful handmade quilts you could imagine for our tiniest two grandbabies.

Leslie, there are no words to express my gratitude for your kindness, creativity, and generosity. Thank you for showing the rest of us how it's done.

Checking in Without Asking a Question

After a close death, you'll sometimes receive countless texts and voicemails ending with a question. For a griever, though, feeling the need to respond to every message can be overwhelming. A text, something like, "Sending love your way," is a kind way to let someone know they're on your heart, without expecting a response.

Reach Out

The Lord has a phenomenal way of giving us a holy nudge when we need it. Act on it. Reaching out doesn't have to be extravagant—a call, an email, or a card to let a friend know they haven't been forgotten will always arrive at the perfect time.

"In you, Lord my God, I put my trust." Psalm 25:1, NIV

What about You?

Do you currently have a grief friend walking alongside you? If so, how have they shown up for you? If you'd like support from someone who understands, but don't currently have anyone filling that role, ask the Lord to send someone. Consider using this space to write about the most meaningful acts of kindness you've received since your loss.

Uncrushed

_____

_____

_____

_____

_____

_____

_____

_____

_____

_____

_____

_____

_____

_____

_____

_____

_____

_____

_____

Beth Marshall

_____

_____

_____

_____

_____

_____

_____

_____

_____

_____

_____

_____

_____

_____

_____

_____

_____

_____

_____

_____

Chapter Twenty-Seven

Prayer Warriors

If you've ever had a day when your grief felt manageable, then from out of nowhere, a wave of emotion washed over you, turning you into an ugly-crying mess in public—that's the perfect day to call in a prayer warrior.

A prayer warrior is someone you can call anytime—day, night, no matter what. They won't judge you or think you're weak, high maintenance, needy, or a burden.

He or she will take your situation straight to the One who created you in the first place.

A prayer warrior won't flippantly respond, "I'll be praying for you," then walk away and forget about you. No, this rare individual is more likely to slam on the brakes, pull off the road, and pray for you right on the side of the interstate.

In catastrophic situations, when your life feels shattered, with no

> *A prayer warrior is someone you can call anytime—day, night, no matter what. They won't judge you or think you're weak, high maintenance, needy, or a burden.*

words to pray, this is the amazing friend who will stand boldly in the gap for you. They will likely reach out to you with an unexpected encouraging text or voice mail at the precise moment you need it. That's what prayer warriors do.

Do You Really Want to Fly Solo?

When I worked in the airline industry, I always loved knowing there were two to three seasoned pilots navigating an all-night transatlantic flight. In bad weather, or when unexpected turbulence came, it was comforting to know there was another highly trained professional pilot on the flight deck ready to help when needed.

> *We were never intended to fly solo through life's best or worst days.*

We were never intended to fly solo through life's best or worst days.

Allowing someone to pray with and for you is an excellent secret weapon on the road toward healing your grief and loving your life again.

Are You a Prayer Warrior?

If so, you are a great gift to this world. Here are a few secrets I want to share about friends who are grieving:

- Just because they're smiling doesn't mean they're not mourning. Most of the time, they have to keep going, even when they feel like they're swimming in peanut butter. (See chapter twelve.)

- *Fine* is a four letter word. If they say it, and you don't think they mean it, you probably need to ask a few more questions.
- They might need to drop off the social media grid for a while, but please keep praying for and checking in with them. They cherish your friendship.
- Over time they may decide to go back to school, learn to play guitar, or even move across the country. Starting new things is a good way for them to keep dreaming and moving forward. Even if they move far away, please keep calling. They need you.
- Most of the world has gone back to their own busy lives, and they get that. The way you continue to reach out on an anniversary, birthday, or other significant day reminds them that they haven't been forgotten.
- Even though they will forever miss their person, they're tougher than they ever thought they could be. They will survive this, and your consistent presence in their life helps them keep going.

"Though one may be overpowered, two can defend themselves. A cord of three strands is not quickly broken." Ecclesiastes 4:12, NIV

How about You?

Is there someone you can call for prayer, any time day or night? I hope there is. If not, that's okay too—you may want to ask the Lord to send a prayer warrior to walk alongside you.

These pages are for writing any specific prayer requests you have. Would you consider reaching out to a faith-filled friend in the next couple days and asking them to pray with and for you? You may be surprised what a difference prayer makes.

Chapter Twenty-Eight

Take the Day Off

Life happens. Calamity comes. Grief sneaks in. And for some reason, we often add more to our already overwhelmed minds, bodies, and souls than we need to.

The world whispers, "Do more, be more, live your best life." But your best life right now might look more like getting a shower and putting on jeans instead of pj pants.

One of the least selfish things you can do while grieving is to *take time for yourself.* Get some fresh air, exercise, and eat some good food.

> *One of the least selfish things you can do while grieving is to take time for yourself. Get some fresh air, exercise, and eat some good food.*

In this "more than I can handle" season, what if you could give yourself a break and take care of you, without feeling compelled to…

- clean out every corner of your home?

- create a Pinterest-worthy home, yard, or meal?
- hang out with exhausting people?
- compete in a CrossFit world championship?
- run a marathon?
- hold yourself to impossible standards?

What if setting aside time for yourself was actually a brilliant step toward healing?

> *"Self-care isn't just drinking water and going to sleep early. Self-care is taking a break when things become overwhelming, saying no to things you do not want to do, allowing yourself to cry, asking for help from those around you, doing things that make you happy."* —*The Mind Journal*

What would it feel like to set your phone on airplane mode and take an entire day off just for you—designated time to breathe, think, rest, and do whatever sounds refreshing to you?

Can you imagine telling your boss, family, and friends you're not going to be available on (you fill in the date)? You won't be taking care of any humans, plants, laundry, pets, carpool lines, tedious meetings…none of it. You're out. I know it sounds extreme, especially if you're used to managing a lot of people and things, but what if the world could keep spinning for twenty-four hours while you got some well-deserved peace and quiet?

You could…

- Go to your happy place—the beach, a park, the mountains, or a hotel, wherever sounds dreamy to you.
- Close your eyes and breathe deeply.

- Take a stroll, instead of a sprint, and take in the creation all around you.
- Eat some creamy delicious, not "lite" ice cream.
- Write a song, paint, sing, or draw.
- Listen to your favorite playlist.
- Watch an *I Love Lucy* rerun—especially the episode where Lucy and Ethyl work on the candy factory assembly line.
- If too much quietness is hard for you, phone a kind, comforting, or seriously funny friend.

"Cry about it, talk about it, write about it, make art about it, move your body about it. It has to go somewhere." —Alex Mammadyarov

Chances are, after taking a day off for yourself, you'll wake up feeling stronger and refreshed.

Whatever energizes you, sparks joy, or even distracts your weary mind for a while—do more of those things.

How about You?

These pages are for dreaming about and planning an entire day off—just for you. What kind of things would you plan to do? Save the date. Get it on the calendar. Let the boss, your spouse, your kids, or anybody else needing to be kept in the loop know that you're taking the day off. Then take it. Ask the Lord to meet you there. You'll be happy you did.

"Don't panic. I'm with you. There's no need to fear for I'm your God. I'll give you strength. I'll help you. I'll hold you steady, keep a firm grip on you." Isaiah 41:10, MSG

Uncrushed

Beth Marshall

_____

_____

_____

_____

_____

_____

_____

_____

_____

_____

_____

_____

_____

_____

_____

_____

_____

_____

Chapter Twenty-Nine

Valentines from Heaven—and
Creating a Memory Box

Just as a grief trigger can come from out of nowhere and take your breath away with the weight of the sorrow, sometimes an unexpected reminder of your beloved person will show up and bring a huge smile to your face.

Growing up in my big family, Christmas and birthdays were a big deal. All five kids loved giving and receiving gifts. But there was one thing that was non-negotiable when a gift would arrive. Practically before the ribbon and wrapping paper hit the ground, a detailed, kind, and prompt thank-you note needed to be penned, addressed, stamped, and ready to send.

I recall a couple times attempting to get by with scribbling a quick thank-you:

Dear ____,
Thank you for the lovely gift.
Love, Beth

As you might imagine, my mindless, generic message would likely get a quick parental veto, and I would be encouraged to come up with something more specific and thoughtful. Thanks, Beazy.

Another correspondence recollection comes from summer camp. Whenever it was time to prep for our summer adventure, our packing list would include clearly labeled color-coordinated clothing, a collapsible camp cup, and plenty of note cards, stamps, and addressed-to-my-mom-and-dad envelopes assembled in a writing kit. It was nearly impossible to neglect sending a note home during rest time at camp.

My family's extreme commitment to correspondence is probably why finding an eighty-four-year-old treasure felt like a gigantic valentine from Heaven.

A valentine from Heaven is a miraculously cool surprise that reminds you of the beloved person you've loved and lost. This divine gift often shows up at the exact moment you need a smile.

As I was cleaning out a cabinet one day, a 6"x9" vinyl notebook turned up from out of nowhere. I don't recall ever seeing it before that day. Just wow. I'd found my mom's (Beazy's) letter-writing kit, created by her mom (Nana) on July 12, 1938 with the priceless inscription, "Have fun—Love you, Mother." They were pretty formal back in the day—not

> *A valentine from Heaven is a miraculously cool surprise that reminds you of the beloved person you've loved and lost. This divine gift often shows up at the exact moment you need a smile.*

Mama or Mom…but Mother. My guess is that, in the summer of 1938, Nana filled this notebook with postage stamps, note cards, and self-addressed-by-Nana envelopes as my mom prepared to leave for summer camp. You can't fight genetics.

Be on the lookout for these kinds of cherished valentines that remind you of your beloved person.

I asked a few social media and IRL (in real life) friends to share any meaningful reminders of the person they've loved and lost.

For my friend Deb, seeing a heart-shaped cloud, a heart-shaped cream on top of a latte, or anything else in the shape of a heart are sweet reminders of the wonderful days with her beautiful mother.

Sherry, her mom, and family always had a special place in their hearts for ladybugs. Now, whenever one of these tiny red-and-black polka-dot creatures lands nearby, her lovely mom comes to mind.

Recently, while looking through an old footlocker in the attic, I came across this beautiful baby girl dress, custom smocked by my mom. Beazy never complained about how much work these tiny works of art were. She must have known they would be worn, loved, and passed down to her great-granddaughters and maybe even *their* great-grands for generations to come.

Memory Box

One excellent way to keep your loved one's life front-and-center in your heart is to create a special place to keep reminders of them. A memory box doesn't have to be fancy or expensive. An old-school camp trunk will work perfectly fine.

Your memory box might include...

- a special fragrance or aftershave
- sentimental clothing items
- notes, cards, or recipes written in their handwriting
- their favorite music or video
- your loved one's Bible
- a journal for writing stories
- encouraging cards, letters, or photos you received from friends
- a cozy blanket

On a particularly difficult day when you're missing your person, you may want to turn on some soothing music, get cozy, and spend a little time going through your memory box. Reminiscing, smiling, laughing, crying, or doing whatever you feel like doing can help you feel close to them.

There are online and in-person companies that will take a recipe, or something else written in your person's handwriting, and turn it into a pillow, wall hanging, or some other kind of keepsake. How cool is that idea?

Kid Grief

Grief is tough for all of us, but it can be particularly difficult for children. If there are kids in your life who are mourning the death of someone they love, a small suitcase can be a comforting place for them to collect and continue adding sentimental reminders. The items in a memory suitcase can be great conversation starters for a child who might not be able to express feelings around the loss. Encourage drawing pictures, re-watching videos, and adding photos and anything else that reminds the child of the person they're missing.

My prayer is that collecting treasured keepsakes for yourself or for a child will stir up memories and spark glimmers of hope.

How about You?

Is a memory box something that sounds helpful? If so, today could be the perfect day to start curating a unique place to reflect and remember your person. Is there something in nature that reminds you of them? If so, I invite you to write about it here. I love how the Lord will continue to remind you, even decades later, of the unique people He placed in your life.

Section Eight

Remembering with Friends

Chapter Thirty

Social Media—Love It or Hate It?

S ocial media is newsy, entertaining, and fun...until it isn't. When life is going wonderfully, social media can be a terrific way to stay connected with people around the globe. And who doesn't love sharing a stunning vacation beach photo that's been perfectly filtered to camouflage unsightly wrinkles, unwanted curves, or family chaos behind the scenes?

> *Social media is newsy, entertaining, and fun...until it isn't.*

But, when your heart is heavy, the seemingly flawless social media images can intensify how hard and messy your life feels right now.

When Social Media Is Your Friend

I love the way my American Widow Project (AWP) friends (chapter twenty-one) leverage social media not only to stay connected but also to support each other and honor their fallen heroes.

When a significant anniversary or birthday is coming up, these courageous women will often post a photo to let family, military friends, and their "widow sisters" know ahead of time that a certain day could be a difficult one.

It's heartwarming to see the AWP social media community rally around each other by posting photos, words of encouragement,

> *But, when your heart is heavy, the seemingly flawless social media images can intensify how hard and messy your life feels right now.*

and sometimes a story the family may have never heard before about their hero.

I'm a big fan of reaching out on social media platforms on important days, to stir up a little conversation not only about the people I'm missing but also to invite online friends to share creative ways *they* remember *their* person. We're all in this together.

For example, I shared this recently on Facebook.

"This week marks the anniversary of my best friend/mom, Beazy's sudden death. She and her handsome, then-newlywed husband, Herb (aka Herbie the Love Bug), were living their best life nestled in the beautiful Blue Ridge Mountains of North Carolina.

Mom passed away in the peak of autumn, her forever favorite season. I'll never forget the extraordinary fall colors that seemed to last for weeks that year.

As the holidays approached, my brothers, sisters, and extended family were left wondering, *what would Beazy* do on these crisp fall days with Thanksgiving just around the corner?

I believe she would…

- turn up the music and cook up all things pumpkin spice.
- make a plan and gather with her closest humans for a fabulous meal and lots of laughs.
- remind us of her signature statement, 'No problem with Beazy.'
- make sure the people she loved most knew it. Every single day.

This week, I plan to celebrate Beazy by stirring up some kind of pumpkin spice creation, listening to the fall leaves crackle under my feet, laughing more, and letting my closest people know how much I love them. That's what Beazy would do.

Shine On, Mom!"

At the end of the post, I invited my social media friends to share in the comments anything fun, memorable, or delicious they do to celebrate their beloved person. The responses were heartwarming. Some friends shared a memory they had with Beazy. Others talked about inspiring and unique ways their families continue to honor their family members.

Legacy Video

My friend Dr. Melanie commented:

"I always embrace the memories, not try to ignore them.

I have a video of my husband reading the Christmas story to my son who was a toddler. Part of our private family Christmas celebration annually is watching it. My husband still shares the Christmas story every year."

Dr. Melanie also shared that when her family was celebrating their last Christmas with her dad, "We all grabbed our phones to record as he started to read the Christmas story, which he always did before we opened gifts."

This lovely legacy video idea inspired me to record a few impromptu Q & A stories with some of our elder family members at this year's Christmas gathering. Thanks for the excellent idea, Dr. Melanie!

A couple other Facebook friends shared delicious legacy recipes their families still love to make during the holidays:

Sherri's Mom's World-Famous Sausage Balls

1 pound sausage, browned
1 1/4 cups Bisquick
8 ounce package of cream cheese
1 cup shredded pepper jack or seriously sharp cheddar
Mix, form into balls. Bake for 25 minutes at 350 degrees. Yummo.

Patti's Mom's Magnificent Chocolate Pie with Meringue

1 1/2 cups sugar
1 1/2 cups milk
4 T flour
4 T Hershey Cocoa
3 egg yolks beaten
Mix and stir in a double boiler until thick. Put in pie shell and bake at 350 degrees for 30 minutes

Meringue

3 egg whites—beat until stiff

1 tsp cream of tartar

1/3 to 2/3 cups sugar (slowly beat in until light and foamy)

Bake at 350 degrees until light brown

Another meaningful social media outreach came from an Instagram grief support account in the weeks leading up to Mother's Day. The followers who were missing their mothers were asked to submit a photo of their mom, along with her favorite song. All the images were combined to create a magnificent online photo collage set to music. This masterpiece was released on Mother's Day as an Instagram story, celebrating moms from all over the world. A sweet photo of my mom, Beazy, along with her favorite "Feeling Groovy" song in the background, was a part of this thoughtful tribute I'll never forget.

All that to say, social media can provide great comfort and companionship for people, even in a difficult time after loss.

On the flip side, it might be time to press pause on social media if you...

- cringe every time you click amid all the seemingly perfect lives
- can't deal with one more loud political opinion
- are exhausted from images of what everyone ate for lunch, daily photos and stats from the gym, or incessant humble-brags about their A+ honor roll student. Did these perfect kids never draw on the wall with a Sharpie? Or cut their own bangs with kindergarten scissors? Or was that just at my house?

Whenever Facebook, Instagram, Twitter, TikTok, or any not-real-life platform becomes more stress-producing than joy-sparking, it might be time to take a step back. These platforms will likely still be there—showcasing the highlight reels, best of the best, and loudest of the loud voices—when and if you decide to give it another go. Or not.

There's no need to apologize for stepping away from situations in real life or on a screen that are creating more anxiety than joy.

> *There's no need to apologize for stepping away from situations in real life or on a screen that are creating more anxiety than joy.*

How about You?

If social media is part of your life, do you love it or hate it? Or both? Are there ways you could invite people in by sharing a story on a social platform? Or maybe you're considering stepping away for a while. These pages are for writing whatever's on your mind.

Beth Marshall

Chapter Thirty-One

Living Legacies

One of the most heartbreaking thoughts when someone dies is imagining their life being forgotten. Creating an ongoing memorial, planting a tree, or orchestrating an event are all excellent ways to show honor and keep a loved one's legacy alive.

Finding a way to continue the passion, work, or goodness of someone's life can bring meaning and joy to those left behind. Thankfully, there's no time limit for establishing a living legacy to honor the unique individual you're missing.

The #LoisLegacy

Dr. Tony Evans is the pastor of Oak Cliff Bible Fellowship in Dallas, Texas. He and his lovely wife, Dr. Lois Evans, would have celebrated their fiftieth anniversary in 2021. Sadly, in January 2020, Lois Evans passed away, after a hard-fought battle with cancer.

Dr. Lois was the founder of the Pastors' Wives Ministry.

She had always loved sending fresh flowers to honor pastors' wives.

On the one-year anniversary of Lois's funeral, her daughter, Chrystal Evans Hurst, shared this loving tribute on social media:

> "It's been a year since we held the services to celebrate my mother's life. One of the things we talked about publicly was her heart for pastors' wives, and we asked that you would honor our mother's memory by encouraging your pastor's wife.
>
> Well…this is still a good idea. Last year was hard for all of us. It was also hard for the churches that serve us and the pastors that teach us…there were many additional unspoken burdens many pastors' wives had to shoulder."

In the tribute to her mom, Chrystal added, "Pastors' wives are often forgotten for their contributions to the ministries they serve…so, *if you're able, send your pastor's wife flowers as encouragement for the year gone by and encouragement for the year to come. Send her a handwritten note.* If you know her personally, call, text or even DM on social media."

> *"The #LoisLegacy will surely continue honoring pastors' wives for years to come. Encouraging your pastor's wife is a good thing to do. And this time of year is a good time to do it."* —*Chrystal Hurst*

A US Military Hero

US Air Force Technical Sergeant Phillip A. Myers served

multiple tours in Italy, Turkey, Iraq, and Kuwait and was described as having "nerves of steel" while serving on the explosive detection team.

Phillip was a loving husband, a devoted dad, and a courageous US military hero. He was respected by those who served alongside him. Sadly, his wife, Aimee, and their two young children received a knock at the door with the heartbreaking news that Phillip had been killed in action in Afghanistan. He had suffered fatal wounds from an improvised explosive device.

At the time Aimee and their kids, Dakota and Kaiden, were living in England, since Phillip's assignment was with the Royal Air Force in Lakenheath, United Kingdom.

Phillip was awarded a Bronze Star Medal, for bravery while serving in Iraq and was the recipient of the 2008 US Air Force Lupia Civil Engineer NCO of the Year Award. Phillip had been promoted from staff sergeant to tech sergeant just days before his death, but unfortunately, he never got to hear the good news.

Words could never adequately describe the shock, sorrow, and grief Phillip's family experienced, even as they began to put the broken pieces of their life back together.

Aimee and the kids later relocated to Anderson, South Carolina, where they became part of NewSpring Church. That's where Aimee and I met. I asked this beautiful Gold Star Wife if she might share some of their stories of love, loss, and life after such a profound tragedy.

In the season following Phillip's death, the Myers family's military friends in England seemed to know exactly what to do without being asked. They stepped up to offer comfort and care for Aimee and the kids in compassionate and practical ways. For two months, Aimee remembers that "friends would just show up—with meals, to take the kids for a while, or to do whatever I needed to be done."

She added that she and the kids talk about Phillip all the time. In her words, "We may never know how many people he saved by his courage. He loved his family and his work!"

"Murph"—A Hero's Living Legacy

People who knew and loved Phillip came up with creative and appropriate physically challenging ways to honor this fierce hero. Every year, the CrossFit community at Electric City CrossFit in Anderson, South Carolina, hosts an annual competition, "The Murph," in Phillip's memory.

Murph is a classic workout known as a Hero WOD (workout of the day) created by CrossFit, to honor the men and women who have fallen in the line of duty. This workout was put together in honor of Navy Lieutenant Michael Murphy, who was killed in action in Afghanistan. Now, people around the country participate in the grueling timed challenge, including a one-mile run, one hundred pull-ups, two hundred push-ups, three hundred air squats, one-mile run—all with a weight vest.

> *"We may never know how many people he saved by his courage. He loved his family and his work!"*
> *—Gold Star Wife, Aimee Myers*

In July 2021, Phillip's fifteen-year-old son, Kaiden, qualified for the World CrossFit Games, where he ranked number seven in the world.

I can't imagine a more fitting way for Kaiden to honor his heroic dad.

International Tribute

In England, every year on Phillip's birthday, there's a memorial run in his honor, where scores of people show up to run and remember this courageous US military hero. The race finishes at the corner of the street named for Phillip: Myers Way.

> *In July 2021, Phillip's fifteen-year-old son, Kaiden, qualified for the World CrossFit Games, where he ranked number seven in the world.*

I asked Aimee if she had any advice for people walking alongside a grieving friend. Her response, "Be the person who's still there long after their loved one dies."

How about You?

Would you be interested in creating a living legacy to honor and celebrate your person? No pressure, but if so, I encourage you to think about what mattered most to them and brainstorm ideas with your closest people. It doesn't matter if your loved one passed away last week, or decades ago, it's never too early or too late to honor their life by creating a lasting tribute.

Uncrushed

Beth Marshall

_____

_____

_____

_____

_____

_____

_____

_____

_____

_____

_____

_____

_____

_____

_____

_____

_____

Chapter Thirty-Two

Honoring Tate and Brinkley—
The Kirbys' Story

One of the most loving living memorials I've ever heard about came from the Kirby family, after their own loss (see chapter twenty-four).

Baby Tate was a precious healthy little guy, only three months and eight days old when his mom and dad got a shocking call from his daycare provider. During his nap, Tate stopped breathing. The next several hours were a whirlwind of racing to the hospital and meeting with doctors, all to find out their beloved baby son was gone.

While words can never begin to touch the gut-wrenching heartache his mom, dad, brother, grandparents, and community felt, Tate's mom and dad determined early on, "This is not going to ruin us."

Infant, child, and pregnancy loss are some of the most intense and isolating experiences a family ever goes through. Families in the hospital are often left alone in their sorrow with no idea where to turn.

In the months following Tate's death, the Kirbys decided there was something they could do to help other parents facing the crushing sorrow of losing a child. Tate's mom and dad, Whitney and Nick, learned about an incredible organization, HopeMommies.org. Hope Mommies was created to support families in the

Infant, child, and pregnancy loss are some of the most intense and isolating experiences a family ever goes through. Families in the hospital are often left alone in their sorrow with no idea where to turn.

immediate time after infant or pregnancy loss. This caring organization provides online Hope Groups as well as private Facebook groups, where bereaved moms can "connect with other women, share stories, receive encouragement, and cling to Hope together."

Additionally, Hope Mommies creates Hope Boxes as a tangible way to express love, provide biblical truth, and invite bereaved women into a community of fellow Hope Moms.

The Kirbys founded a Hope Mommies chapter that has provided Hope Boxes for over two hundred families so far. These beautiful keepsake boxes include a Bible, a devotional, a journal, and a bath bomb for moms, as well as cards for making handprints and footprints. The Hope Boxes that are given in honor of Tate and his sister Brinkley (see story below), also include a heartfelt note from Whitney.

Whitney's Note:

Dear Hope Mommy,

I am so sorry you are receiving this box. This box represents deep loss. I have experienced this pain you are going through right now. In 2016, my 3 month old son, Tate, passed away at daycare in his sleep. In 2019, my daughter Brinkley was stillborn at 29 weeks gestation. I understand your feelings of despair and sadness. After my losses, I felt so alone and scared for the future. This box was made through an organization called "Hope Mommies." There is a whole army of women who have lived through this loss and are praying for you as you walk this road. I give this box to you in hopes that it will bring some peace and love to a dark time. I pray that you know you are loved and you are not alone. I am here for you if you would ever like to talk.

Love, Whitney

In addition to creating Hope Boxes, the local chapter the Kirbys founded purchased a comfy rocker and ottoman for parents to sit and rock their child, while in the hospital. Whitney, Nick, and their living children, Hudson, Charlie, and Harper, wanted to make sure that Tate and Brinkley's lives made a difference.

One scripture that has been especially meaningful to the Kirby family comes from Hebrews 6:19, NLT.

"This hope is a strong and trustworthy anchor for our souls. It leads us through the curtain into God's inner sanctuary."

Tate and Brinkley, your legacy is absolutely touching brokenhearted families with the love of Christ.

Shine on, precious little ones.

If you or someone you know has experienced the heartbreak of infant or pregnancy loss, I pray that the Lord will meet you exactly where you are, surround you with people who understand, and comfort you as only He can, by Jesus' mighty power. Amen.

To seek help, or learn how to get involved with this caring organization, I invite you to visit the HopeMommies.org website.

Section Nine

Staying Uncrushed

Chapter Thirty-Three

Breathe Through Your Nose, and Wiggle Your Toes

Expressing exactly what your loved one meant to you can be challenging.

My dear friend Dorothy's dad was a beloved pediatric dentist. Dr. C's sudden death rocked Dorothy, her family, and everyone who knew him to the very core.

I was introduced to Dorothy in a most unusual way. She and I lived in a relatively small community in South Carolina, and we shared several mutual friends. Dorothy's light and life radiated joy to those around her, so it was no surprise to hear that she had been surrounded by lots of caring friends in the wake of her dad's death.

The year of Dr. C's death, my *Grief Survivor* book had just been released, and apparently, a few early copies had landed in the hands of some local friends. News travels fast in the small town.

Barely forty-eight hours after Dr. C's tragic death, as Dorothy and her family continued reeling from the shock, likely having to remind themselves to breathe, someone dropped a copy of the new grief book at her door. My understanding is that she looked at the title, shook her head, and proceeded to sling the book across the room like a frisbee. Boy, do I get that. I probably would have done the same thing.

A week later, another friend sent Dorothy a copy. Then, two weeks later, a third copy of my grief book landed in her mailbox.

Grief Friend to Real-Life Friend

As Dorothy tells it, "That's when I thought, okay, I get it. Maybe I should open the (#%@&) book." After hearing about several people reaching out to Dorothy with the book—especially the frisbee part—I asked our mutual friend Laura if she might introduce us. After all, everybody loved Dorothy. She and I met for coffee, and eight years later, I consider her one of the dearest people I know.

I love how God sometimes turns a grief friendship into a real-life friendship.

> *I love how God sometimes turns a grief friendship into a real-life friendship.*

—and our friendship is one of the most precious to me.

Then in the spring of 2020, right smack in the early days of the COVID-19 pandemic, she became a newlywed!

Back to the Story

Dorothy's dad, Dr. C, had the most brilliant solution for when

258

one of his pint-sized dental patients felt anxious. He'd remind them to "Breathe through your nose, and wiggle your toes."

Try it. It's impossible to continue freaking out when you're breathing through your nose and wiggling your toes at the same time. This clear and calming message became a heartwarming eight-word tribute to Dorothy's lovable dad. I wish I'd known Dr. C when I was the kid freaking out in a dental chair!

> *"Breathe through your nose, and wiggle your toes."*

In the years since losing her dad, Dorothy has gathered lots of insight. Here are a few of my favorite Dorothy quotes:

- After hearing an insensitive and ridiculous remark from a well-meaning person—"Heaven doesn't need another angel."
- "In times of grief, we've got to remember that the decision we're making today doesn't have to be the decision forever."
- "Take a break from social media."
- "Do the best you can today...and maybe don't do the best you can—it's okay."
- "God is so much bigger, more graceful, more loving, and awesome than I had ever given Him credit for."
- "Even in my confusion...God was there all along."

And whenever life is just too hard, remember Dr. C's wise words: "Breathe through your nose, and wiggle your toes."

I love how his kind and winsome spirit still shines brightly through his lovely daughter Dorothy.

Live, Love, Laugh, Repeat

My mom was one of the most optimistic humans ever created. She could spin a hard situation into a silver lining faster than an Olympic athlete. While I could write volumes about her humor and love for life, one day I tried to bring all the words down to

> *"God is so much bigger, more graceful, more loving, and awesome than I had ever given Him credit for."*
> —Dorothy Camak Jenkins

just a few and to describe her legacy in a nutshell. Here's what I came up with: "She taught us to live, love, laugh, repeat!" Can you see why we still miss her?

"God can do anything, you know—far more than you could ever imagine or guess or request in your wildest dreams! He does it not by pushing us around but by working within us, his Spirit deeply and gently within us." Ephesians 3:20, MSG

How about You?

Absolutely no pressure here, but consider using these pages to write about your person's legacy with seven to eight carefully curated words to describe them.

Hopefully, this phrase will be a meaningful reminder of why your beloved person's life is much too important to be forgotten.

Beth Marshall

_____

_____

_____

_____

_____

_____

_____

_____

_____

_____

_____

_____

_____

_____

_____

_____

_____

_____

_____

Uncrushed

Chapter Thirty-Four

Looking for Goodness

S ome years are definitely tougher than others, especially
when crippling adversity or loss have been part of their
story. You may be an avid bucket list planner. If so, looking
to the future is a wonderful way to start dreaming big again.

During a difficult year, though, looking back can also be
a valuable tool for drawing attention to the good things that
have taken place, even in the midst of a not-so-terrific time.

Reverse Bucket List

"The reverse bucket list is pretty straightforward: Rather
than writing down all the things you hope to one day
achieve, you instead write down a list of all the things
you've already accomplished, things that make you feel
proud. It's the exact opposite of a regular bucket list—and
it's an encouraging exercise." —Anna Meyer-Shine

My friend Nicki Koziarz has experienced a lot of loss in
recent years. Especially heartbreaking were the deaths of
her brother and her mom. Even through these seasons of

unthinkable sorrow, Nicki continued to inspire others through writing and speaking for Proverbs 31 Ministries and hosting her *Lessons from the Farm* podcast. In episode 55, "Gratitude When Things Don't Go Our Way," Nicki encourages her listeners to create a reverse bucket list. This list is a slight twist on a traditional reverse bucket list, as she models celebrating blessings that have come, even through dark days, and seeing them all through the lens of God's goodness.

It's heartwarming to hear how people, even after great loss, have managed to create beautiful music, write insightful books, learn new things, and even grow their families—all excellent material for a reverse bucket list!

A few wonderful blessings from the past couple years for my family:

My Reverse Bucket List

- welcoming two beautiful healthy babies to our extended family
- completing Book Proposal Bootcamp. Thank you, Coach Nicki Koziarz!
- attending Bob Goff's Writer's Workshop
- the opportunity to write this book!

Joy Triggers

In earlier chapters, we talked about grief triggers and how hard it can be to ride those unpredictable waves.

But what if there were also things, places, or people that catch you off guard with unexpected smiles? Joy triggers?

This morning, I came across a thirty-plus-year-old treasure. It was my grandmom Nana's, favorite perfume, *Interlude,* on a shelf in my closet. Feeling a little nostalgic, I decided to spray on a tiny splash of her signature scent. As I visited and revisited my wrist to catch a whiff, my first thought was, *Interlude is one powerful fragrance.* But then I realized that's probably what my kids and grands think about my favorite fragrance, *Amazing Grace!* I loved how quickly a scent could trigger unexpected joy and memories of my super sweet-smelling Nana.

> *But what if there were also things, places, or people that catch you off guard with unexpected smiles? Joy triggers?*

What Triggers Joy for You?

Your joy triggers might not be a reminder of your beloved person but might be something entirely unrelated that makes you smile. Something as simple as…

- crispy clean sheets
- a delicious meal with your favorite people
- snuggles with a child or tiny baby
- a refreshing swim on a steamy summer day
- a breathtaking sunrise or sunset
- an unexpected act of kindness
- sunshine hitting your face on a cool winter morning

Even in the midst of intense heartache, staying mindful of the little things around you can bring a smile, even if only for a moment.

Grief Is a Thief

Grieving can feel like someone broke into your home and stole some of your valuables during the night. Maybe your energy was stolen? Mental clarity? Restful sleep? Friends? Peace of mind? Confidence to be around humans? Joy? Yep. I get it. Me too.

Grief is a thief, but the thief doesn't get the last word.

While I don't know your pain or your story, I want to encourage you that one day, you will likely reclaim a lot of what's been stolen from you.

A tangible way to acknowledge what stolen goods have already been restored is to revisit what you wrote in the beginning pages of this book or in your journal. Even if it seems you still have miles to go on the broken road toward healing, looking back will help you acknowledge how far you've already come.

> *Grief is a thief, but the thief doesn't get the last word.*

Shower the People You Love with Love

Losing an important piece of your life puzzle is often a wake-up call for how very precious life is and also a sweet reminder to hug our people a little tighter. Being fully present with our closest family and friends is one of the best ways to show appreciation for those we still have here on earth. Another favorite reminder that I could use every day is to

"*Be where your feet are.*" —Bob Goff

In other words, give one hundred percent to the person right in front of you, rather than letting your mind wander off to whatever or whomever is next on the agenda.

The Letter

About a year before my sister-in-law Kay died, I got a gentle nudge in my spirit to *write her a letter* and tell her how much I loved and appreciated her. I wish I could tell you I follow through one hundred percent when one of these spirit-whispers comes, but thankfully, that day I felt with certainty it was time to draft a love note. Little did I know how thankful I would one day be for following through.

Here's a little excerpt from the letter:

Dearest Kay,

I want you to know how awesome I think you are. For real, it's so incredible to have a sister-in-law who is more like a sister, who has lived through decades of family calamities, and keeps laughing through it all. You are showing me what real courage is all about.

My prayer is for the Lord to keep shining His bright light on and through you. I love the way He is on call 24/7, works the night shift, and is always just a prayer away.

I love you, my sister

—Beth

You will never ever regret telling a dear family member or close friend how much they mean to you.

How about You?

Here are a few ideas you might want to think about.

A reverse bucket list—Are there any unexpected blessings or accomplishments you've experienced in recent months or years? A new friendship? Connecting with a person or group who understands what you're going through? A new hobby or career you're enjoying?

> *You will never ever regret telling a dear family member or close friend how much they mean to you.*

Joy triggers—What kinds of everyday goodness feel like warm sunshine sneaking through the cracks of a cloudy day for you?

A letter to someone you love—Close your eyes for a moment, and think about someone in your life right now who might need a little encouragement. Handwritten notes are a bit of a lost art, which, to me, makes them even more valuable.

Shower the people you love with love—Never miss an opportunity to tell a family member or friend how much they mean to you, even if you think they already know.

I invite you to use these pages to follow any of these prompts.

Beth Marshall

Chapter Thirty-Five

What Now?

S o how do you know if you're making progress on this
messy journey called grief? I remember going through seasons where a trigger would wipe me out or tears would come
from out of nowhere. I'd wonder if it was always going to be
this way. I'm happy to tell you that, thankfully, *it won't always
be this way.*

A few glimmers of healing you might be noticing now:

- Sadness and sorrow are not the very first thoughts on
  your mind in the morning.
- Rather than sprinting away from a friend who's
  experiencing adversity, you consider walking toward
  them to offer support and encouragement.
- More smiles and fewer tears.
- "Grief brain" is subsiding. Clarity, focus, and energy
  are slowly returning.
- You're beginning to trust the process and believe hope,
  healing, and maybe even new purpose are possible.
- You're saying yes to more things.
- You're starting to dream about the future again.

Lizzy's Definition of Healing

Remember Mandy, the thirty-two-year-old widow and single mom from chapter twenty-one? Her daughter, Lizzy, was eleven years old when she lost her dad, Zac.

About a year later, I was talking to Lizzy about school and what life looked like for her now. We somehow got on the subject of her thoughts about healing.

Lizzy shared a story about the day she heard about a classmate who had also lost a close loved one. When she heard the news, rather than running away from her heartbroken friend, like she would have done earlier in her journey, she felt more like running toward her. Lizzy wanted to let her friend know that it wouldn't always be this hard.

This wise-beyond-her-years young girl added, "That's probably what healing looks like."

Lizzy's definition of healing is one of the best I've ever heard. I love that she could sense her heart gradually pivoting from one hundred percent inward focus to a place of wanting to use her story to help someone else understand brighter days are coming.

"He comforts us in all our troubles so that we can comfort others. When they are troubled, we will be able to give them the same comfort God has given us." 2 Corinthians 1:4, NLT

> ***"The goal [of grief] is to move through and give yourself permission to have a beautiful meaningful life." —Dr Chloe***

Handprints on Your Heart

Even after unthinkable loss, there's one thing that can never ever be taken away from you—a handprint on your heart. The handprint I'm talking about is the unique difference your person made in your life—their sense of humor, quirkiness, kindness, unconditional love, artistic or musical gifting...the list goes on and on.

On a personal note, I'd love to share a few of the handprints some of my favorite family heroes made on my heart. Hopefully, they will stir up some ideas for celebrating the person you're missing.

Beazy (mom)—Thank you for teaching us to look for wonder and goodness all around us and for being the greatest life-cheerleader a girl could have ever imagined. Thanks to you delicious recipes, fresh cut flowers, and mountain lakes continue to inspire your kids, grandkids, and now your great-grands. I admire how you treated every single person, especially those who were different from us, with genuine respect and love. Thank you for modeling that people are, and will always be, more important than things—even when one of your kids carved "I LOVE MOMY" on your mahogany table.

Kay (sister-in-love)—You were one in a million and always made me feel more like a sister than an in-law. There was always room for one more person at your table. Thank you for the way you loved people, especially grandpeople, with your whole heart. In your final battle with illness, you showed the world what fierce courage and grace look like. Thank you for always making us laugh—even on the hardest days.

"Almost without exception the most beautiful, selfless people I've met are the ones who've experienced personal tragedy." —Donald Miller

How about You?

At this point on your road toward healing, are you seeing glimpses of what Lizzy experienced the day her focus began to shift outward, where she showed up for a grieving friend?

Are there character traits, hobbies, or other parts of your loved ones' stories that you hope will always be part of your life?

Do you believe the Lord is able to restore your hope and purpose—and your understanding that it's okay to smile and live your life again?

> *One of the most honoring things we can do after going through a hard journey of mourning is to find ways to keep living our lives with joy and purpose.*

One of the most honoring things we can do after going through a hard journey of mourning is to find ways to keep living our lives with joy and purpose.

I invite you to use this space for your thoughts around healing through grief. Also, consider describing some of the unique handprints your loved one left on your heart.

Beth Marshall

Chapter Thirty-Six

Starting to Dream Again

G etting back into life.
    Starting something new.
Ask the Lord what's the next thing He has for you.

Dreaming Big

Sometimes life's most difficult times become the catalyst for starting something entirely new. A couple of the American Widow Project ladies talked about their new dreams of moving cross-country or learning to play guitar. For others, like my friend LuAnn, her next bold new step was creating the Blooming Again grief support group.

In the wake of the crushing death of her beloved husband, Clay, my friend Kristy wanted to find a way to honor his life and to help other hurting people.

In Kristy's words, "God is designing a beautiful tapestry from our lives. We are *cloth* in His hands. Right now, we only see threads and colors. We see the back of the tapestry and we can't imagine what the Artist is creating on the other side. But, when we get to Heaven, we will see the finished work in all its beauty. In that moment, Jesus will reveal the beauty He was creating with our lives. Everything will make sense."

Shortly after Clay's death, Kristy purchased a lovely property in St. Francisville, Louisiana that's now called "The Hill." The lovely Victorian home has been transformed into a retreat center for people experiencing loss, tragedy, and sorrow to find comfort and healing. Not a moment of Kristy's pain has been wasted.

Your dreams will surely look completely different from other peoples' dreams, but the point is giving yourself permission to dream again and to know that your story is not over yet.

"Surround yourself with people who would shout your name in a room full of opportunities." —Thrive.com

Coming Full Circle

Remember our Aussie friend Josh from chapter nine? Here's an inspiring bit of follow-up and how he continues to honor his beautiful mum by reaching out to others. In his words, "I've learned some things along the way. By no means am I an expert, but it has become a key part of my story and will forever be."

Josh recently launched a podcast called *Narrative Society.* He describes this new work as "a little attempt to shine some light and hopefully help anyone going through a painful season."

In addition to Josh's new podcast, he created these quick steps in his griever's toolbox:

Quick Steps

- **Ask for help.** You don't have to go through it alone.
- **Don't hide.** Be honest with your close friends about how you're doing.
- **Be honest.** You don't have to fake it. It can be really tough. Lose the mask.
- **Buy a journal.** Capture your memories and scribble your thoughts.
- **Counseling.** Go see a professional counselor. It is so helpful.

"You don't need the right words when someone goes through grief, heartache, and pain— you just need to be present." —*Josh Bull*

Josh's podcast is a beautiful image of Ephesians 3:20 and God's mighty power to work in us to accomplish extraordinary things—even beyond our wildest dreams!

How about You?

Is there a dream coming to your mind right now or something you would be excited to do in the season ahead? Maybe you've always wanted to learn a new language, travel to Antarctica, or learn to fly an airplane. What is a first step you could take this week to make your dream become a reality?

_____

_____

_____

_____

_____

_____

_____

_____

_____

_____

_____

_____

_____

_____

_____

_____

_____

_____

Beth Marshall

_____

_____

_____

_____

_____

_____

_____

_____

_____

_____

_____

_____

_____

_____

_____

_____

_____

Chapter Thirty-Seven

Taking Back Your Life

G rief and loss can feel confusing as we begin taking steps toward what's next, while not wanting to move away from the person that we're missing.

Transformed Grief

It's hard to put into words what transformed grief would look like for you, since I probably never had the honor of knowing your beloved person. One thing I'm noticing in my journey of love, loss, and healing is that my deep, sometimes debilitating, pain has gradually transformed into profound thankfulness for the dear ones who are no longer here. The same is possible for you, my friend.

> *But God, in His infinite wisdom is somehow able to take our sorrow, adversity, or trauma and transform the pain to new purpose, by His mighty healing power.*

If you had told me years ago that instead of wrangling rambunctious first graders or flying across the ocean on jumbo jets I would be writing my third grief-related book...with all due respect, I would have thought you had lost your mind.

But God, in His infinite wisdom is somehow able to take our sorrow, adversity, or trauma and transform the pain to new purpose, by His mighty healing power.

He is fully able to do the same for you. I promise.

Pain to Purpose

My friend Davey Blackburn, in the years since the traumatic death of his beloved wife, Amanda, likely experienced days where he wasn't sure the sun would ever peek through the clouds again, for him and his toddler son, Weston.

Several years and lots of healing later—Davey is now the founder of Nothing is Wasted Ministries, creator of the Pain to Purpose Course, and host of the Nothing Is Wasted podcast.

In Davey's Words

"Your dent in your life doesn't have to become your identity. Your test can become a great testimony. Your mess can become your greatest message." —Davey Blackburn

Over time, Davey has been abundantly blessed to find love again. He and Kristi were married several years ago and have built a beautiful life with their three children, Weston, Natalia, and Cohen.

"Davey and Kristi have journeyed together through a story of tragedy and triumph, of pain and of purpose, and

their hope for the future lies firmly in Christ. This couple's trust and faith in Jesus shows their eagerness to share with the world His message of healing, of hope, and of the truth that Nothing Is Wasted." —NothingIsWasted.com

Open to Hope

Dr. Gloria Horsley and her daughter, Dr. Heidi Horsley, experienced unbearable sorrow with the tragic death of Gloria's son, and Heidi's brother, Scott.

Over the years, the Horsleys have allowed their unimaginable sorrow to be transformed into purpose. This compassionate mother-daughter team co-founded a lovely non-profit, Open to Hope. Their online content currently provides articles, videos, and endless support for their compassionate grief community around the world.

"We've been there before and we are here to help you; if you've lost hope, lean on ours until you find your own." —Dr. Gloria and Dr. Heidi Horsley

Dear friend, while I don't know where you are on your path, I encourage you to watch for light and hope beginning to peek through the dark, the way Davey, Dr. Gloria, and Dr. Heidi have. Their pain-to-purpose stories remind me *that there is always hope.*

Both/And

Grief is a strange thing where contrasting emotions show up simultaneously. Even though it's been a while since losing my mom, my dad, my grandmom Nana, and sister-in-law Kay, I can still get teary when I hear a song they loved, catch a whiff of their favorite scent, or see a forgotten old photo.

At the same time, those moments can bring a wave of thankfulness for the phenomenal people who will forever be in my heart.

You may be feeling confusion alongside great clarity, intense pain along with hopefulness, or other conflicting emotions. I want to remind you to hold space for all of it. Roll with whatever waves come your way, rather than trying to fight them.

How about You?

Instead of comparing your progress, and thinking you're not coping as well as someone else, what if you reframed that thought to, "If they can do it, so can I"?

If you're not feeling as far down the road as the people in these stories, that is perfectly fine. Your story and relationship with your person is like no other.

Instead of comparing your progress, and thinking you're not coping as well as someone else, what if you reframed that thought to, "If they can do it, so can I"?

These pages are for writing about your big dreams, small dreams, or whatever came to mind as you read these pain-to-purpose stories.

Beth Marshall

Chapter Thirty-Eight

Remember, Rest, and Reach Out

R emember
  Here are a few things to remember—some we've talked about, others we haven't—as you navigate the unpredictable waters of grief.

It's *never too late* to start processing and healing your grief. If it's been a long time since losing your dear person, going through old letters, photos, scrapbooks, or videos can help you stir up memories and encourage you to write about them. Writing about my beloved family members has been an important stone on the pathway toward healing my grief and restoring my joy.

Everybody goes through loss in their own way, at their own pace. If kids, sisters, brothers, parents, a spouse, or friends approach loss differently than you—tears or no tears, hyper or needing lots of sleep, anxious or calm—it's all okay. We're all doing the best we can.

Instead of waiting for people to show up for you, *invite them in.* If you're feeling forgotten or isolated today, consider calling a friend. Often people would love to be there for us but don't know what we need.

Say what you need to say to the people you love most. Cherish them. Make memories. Keep short accounts. Forgive quickly.

> *Say what you need to say to the people you love most. Cherish them. Make memories. Keep short accounts. Forgive quickly.*

Rest

Rest is not laziness. It's not irresponsible. In fact, it's holy. *God rested.* He worked like crazy for six days creating the heavens and earth, and light, and darkness, and land, and seas, and every form of plant and tree and fruit, and the sun and the moon, and the galaxies, and fish. And that was in just four days. Then, He started creating every imaginable kind of animal, and humans, and He told them to be fruitful and multiply, and they did.

"Then God looked over all he had made, and he saw that it was very good!" Genesis 1:31a, NLT

And then, *"And God blessed the seventh day and declared it holy, because it was the day when he rested from all his work of creation."* Genesis 2:3, NLT

God rested. So can we.

Reaching Out to a Grieving Friend

- Don't try to make it better, fix it, fill the awkward silence with words, or tell them how they should or shouldn't feel.

- Check in and keep checking in, not just in the first few weeks, but years down the road.
- Be intentional to note important dates on your calendar.
- Be curious. Ask questions about their loved one. You'll know if they're ready to talk. If not, that's okay too.
- Saying their person's name reminds them of the impact they made in your life too.
- Keep calling, texting, and inviting them.
- One of the kindest things you can do for a grieving friend is to "hold space" for them.

> *To hold space is to be all in for them—emotionally, mentally, and physically—and allow them to feel whatever they're feeling.*

To hold space is to be all in for them—emotionally, mentally, and physically—and allow them to feel whatever they're feeling.

"Let us hold unswervingly to the hope we profess, for he who promised is faithful." Hebrews 10:23, NIV

Chapter Thirty-Nine

What I Wish Someone Had Told Me

When Grief Was Fresh

"There's a fear I have. When their name is not said I worry they are forgotten. There is a great joy I have when their name is said...to know they are remembered." —The Grief Toolbox

Even on days you're feeling anxious, tearful, isolated, numb, achy like you have the flu, or hopeless—you're not crazy. You are grieving. You've lost a dear part of your life, and the pain you're feeling seems unbearable. It won't always be this hard.

Write. Write. Write. Writing about the person, or people, you're missing helps you to slow down, to deep dive into the emotions, and to begin to heal. Writing builds confidence that their unique story will not be forgotten.

When traumatic loss comes and disrupts your life, you may not have the words or strength to pray. Lean on a friend's faith and hope 'til you find your own again. You can trust God, His love, and His word. He is who He says He is—Jehovah Rapha, God who heals.

Let people in. *Say yes* to kind offers of support.

One day you'll see a wave coming, or maybe not see it coming, and it will wash over you, but it won't have the power to take you under anymore.

What if your story becomes a life raft for someone feeling isolated and forgotten?

As healing continues, consider saying yes...

- to invitations for dinner with friends, parties, showers, events, and life
- to sharing your story
- to being available for someone whose grief is fresh and raw

Loving life again doesn't mean that you don't still miss your beloved person like crazy. It just means you're beginning to heal.

Plan things to look forward to in the future—a new hobby, a business venture, seeing a Broadway play, or whatever sounds fun to you.

Invite older relatives to tell their stories about childhood, their favorite job, or the most awesome vacation ever. Make a video of their stories. You'll be glad you did.

Look at your life honestly, and identify the ways you've grown and healed.

Look for God winks—tiny, or not-so-tiny, unexplained miracles—and write about them in your journal.

Feeling joy does not mean you're not still missing your loved one. It means that you are human and really will be able to love your life again.

What I Would Have Told Myself

Ten days before Beazy's death, she and I had the most unexpected and glorious time together. A family beach trip had been canceled, due to a hurricane warning. The rest of the family opted to stay home, so I headed to the mountains for a long weekend with Beazy. I had no idea it would be the last time I'd see her this side of Heaven.

> *Feeling joy does not mean you're not still missing your loved one. It means that you are human and really will be able to love your life again.*

If I had known then what I know now, here's the letter I would have written to myself:

Dear Beth,

This weekend with Beazy is a gift from the Lord. You might not see it now, but one day these lovely moments on her wraparound porch, overlooking the Blue Ridge Mountains, seeing her living her best life ever will be an image you'll never want to forget.

One day you'll understand what a precious treasure that impromptu solo visit was, as you and Beazy enjoyed walks on the crunchy autumn leaves, cooked yummy food together, and laughed 'til you cried.

You probably want to go ahead and tell her how thankful you are that God picked her to be your mom. And that her belly laugh is one of the sweetest sounds ever created. And thank her for always believing in you, and being on your team, no matter what.

Go ahead and hug her really hard. If you could, you'd never let her go.

In ten days, you're going to get a phone call that will change your life forever. Today's the last time you'll see her sparkly blue eyes, this side of Heaven.

I'm not writing this to scare you but to remind you that you're tougher than you ever thought you were. You will get through this, and you will be stronger on the other side.

I know it sounds crazy now, but one day you'll write books to help other heartbroken people remember the amazing person they're missing. Crazy, right?

Beazy's story will hopefully be a bright light to help lots of people find healing, hope, and great joy again.

Hang on tight, girl. You know Beazy would be smiling right now and reminding you, "Everything's going to work out. It always does."

Love, Beth

"*He heals the brokenhearted and binds up their wounds.*" Psalm 147:3, NIV

"*There's no greater gift in grief than to ask them about their loved one. Then, really listen.*" *—Geneva Livingstone*

How about You?

What do you wish someone had told you? Are there any grief tips you've picked up along the way? Additionally, what would you say to your former self the day or days before your loved one died? These pages are the perfect place to write yourself a letter, or anything else that might be helpful today.

Beth Marshall

_____

_____

_____

_____

_____

_____

_____

_____

_____

_____

_____

_____

_____

_____

_____

_____

_____

_____

Chapter Forty

Living Uncrushed

At this point, you might be feeling a long way down the road toward healing, restored joy, and being one hundred percent ready to conquer the world. That is awesome! I pray you will keep finding ways to honor and celebrate your loved one's life, as you keep dreaming about what's next for you.

But for others, you may know there will never be a big beautiful bow on the package or a diploma stating your grief journey is complete. The hole in your heart left by your missing loved will always exist on this side of eternity. There's absolutely no shame if that describes you right now.

I encourage you to take time to reflect on exactly what you've been through and how it has affected your life and relationships so far. Great loss, for many of us, becomes a huge marker, the moment that separates life before and life after your dear one's death.

I pray that as you keep moving forward on your journey, you'll continue to make space to sit quietly and write—the good, bad, the crazy, all of it—and that the Lord will meet you exactly where you are. May He wash over you with His peace, joy, and the continued healing He has begun in your life.

"And I am certain that God, who began the good work within you, will continue his work until it is finally finished on the day when Christ Jesus returns." Philippians 1:6, NLT

Wise Closing Words

Remember Mandy from chapters twenty-one and twenty-two—the lovely friend who became a widow and single mom in an instant, at age thirty-two, the moment her beloved husband, Zac, died? While the road has been rocky and hard, Mandy has traveled the past ten years with her three—now grown—kids with grace, vulnerability, and grit.

One of my favorite Mandy quotes is:

> *"Grief is not a sign of weakness or lack of faith, but the consequence of awesome love. And that's okay." —Mandy Smith*

My Prayer for You

May the Lord use your unique healing story as a cool drink of water for someone else who has experienced profound loss. He really is able to create a new song in your heart, where there was deep sadness. I pray you will be on the lookout for glimmers of light and hope shining down on your path.

He sees you, He loves you, and He is fully able to turn your darkness into dancing and bring back the finger-painting-with-chocolate-pudding (or whatever that looks like in your life) person you've been missing.

Let It Be So, Lord!
Grace and peace, Beth Marshall

"The Lord bless you and keep you;
the Lord make his face shine on you and be gracious to you;
the Lord turn his face toward you and give you peace."
Numbers 6:24-26, NIV

Bonus Chapters

The content in these bonus chapters may or may not be relevant to what you're going through, but I invite you to check them out, in case you know someone else they might help.

Bonus Chapter One

When You See It Coming— Anticipatory Grief

I t's tough to say which is harder, losing someone suddenly— with absolutely no time to brace—or the gradual process when you see it coming. Either way, there's no easy way out.

My husband, Paul, and I were both blessed with amazing moms with pretty unique names. You've heard lots of Beazy stories in these pages, but let me introduce you to my mother-in-love Mozelle, better known as "Mozie." Awesome names, right? Welcome to the South.

Our (ten-year-old at the time) daughter Amy pretty much nailed describing Mozie in this *Rockin' with My Grandma* poem.

Rockin' with My Grandma

When I rock with my Grandma it's never in a chair.
It's always something active like dancing with no care.

She likes to rock from morning to night: she's always right on beat.

She never ever stops to complain about her weary feet!

The jitterbug and cha cha suit her really fine,
but she loves the macarena and dancing in a line.

In the summer you might spot her swimming at the pool,
but all the other seasons she thinks hiking's pretty cool.

My grandma is never lazy, she's lots of fun of course.
She even taught my brother how to ride a horse.

She'll play when it is sunny. She'll play when it is damp,
because being at my grandma's is like going to summer
camp.

We don't go over the river, we just go through the woods,
knowing that we'll have a great time in Mozie's
neighborhood.

Amy Marshall

The Longest Dance

When Mozie was in her seventies she began to struggle to
come up with words. Sometimes she couldn't remember if
she'd had lunch or not. We didn't think much of it. Everybody
has moments where you walk into a room and can't remember why you're there, right? Mozie still loved to swim, sneak
chocolate from her hidden Hershey's stash, go for walks, play
bridge, and do many of the things she'd always done.

I remember Mozie one day, tilting her head and gently hitting herself above the ear, and saying, "I wish I could knock
this cloudiness out of my head."

Our family was not surprised, but still crushed, when the

doctors ultimately confirmed that her declining memory was attributed to Alzheimer's. As the disease progressed, little bits of her extraordinary life faded away right before our eyes.

Mozie's family was determined to walk this difficult road with the same care and compassion she had always poured out on us.

Whenever she would get facts confused, instead of correcting her, it was always a better option to "just go with it." We were reminded daily that *being kind is way more important than being right* (always), but especially when someone's facing memory challenges. Confrontation would make her anxious, so why go down that road?!

Sparking Moments of Joy

As the Alzheimer's progressed, Mozie's memory of recent events became pretty foggy. But, if you asked her about her handsome WWII Naval officer hero, Stan, back in the 1940s serving in the South Pacific, she was clear as day!

It was always fun taking a walk down memory lane with Mozie. Anything thirty-plus years ago was fair game. Here are a couple favorite memories we loved to stir up:

First, when Stan saw this stunning sixteen-year-old walking down the stairs in high heels, he boldly declared to Mozie's brother Rex, "I'm gonna marry that girl!" Brother Rex quickly replied, "The heck you say!" A few years later, Stan not only married that pretty girl, but five kids and fourteen grandkids later, was still madly in love with her! Mozie never tired of sharing that sweet love story.

Another beautiful memory took place weeks before our

wedding. My husband, Paul, called from Boston to tell Mozie and Stan in South Carolina that we may have to postpone our wedding. There were complications with the original wedding venue in Atlanta.

Without blinking an eye, Mozie offered to *host our wedding*. Three weeks later, in their lovely garden, Paul and I, along with thirty-five of our closest people, enjoyed the most unforgettable wedding day. Our wedding angel had taken care of every detail from scrumptious catering, to chocolate and caramel bride and groom cakes, to orchestrating the Hawaiian Wedding Song sung by her sister Bessie, and even daisies for my hair!

Hospitality and fun were her superpowers!

Whenever we stepped back in time, Mozie was no longer a confused elderly woman battling a wretched disease. She was the sassy sixteen-year-old in high heels charming a handsome boy!

While her long dance with Alzheimer's was incredibly hard, we were deeply grateful for all the precious time with Mozie and being able to celebrate her extraordinary life.

Remembering KK

The months following my sister-in-law Kay's brain cancer diagnosis were full of every emotion possible—clinging to any encouraging thought that a cure might come quickly, while subconsciously bracing ourselves for what we feared would happen. And when do you stop hoping and let your precious loved one know they don't have to keep fighting?

While our family definitely leaned toward any optimistic

outcome, we all sensed that Kay's days this side of eternity were numbered. The tension between hope and letting go was palpable.

Anticipatory grief isn't discussed much in our culture, but for some families, this strange in-between season can be a sweet opportunity to have important conversations, offer and receive forgiveness, and have a (sometimes really long) moment to say goodbye.

> *...this strange in-between season can be a sweet opportunity to have important conversations, offer and receive forgiveness, and have a (sometimes really long) moment to say goodbye.*

Silver Linings

I know it might sound crazy, but there are a few things our family experienced during Kay's eighteen-month illness that were not all sad and terrible. A few silver linings I recall were...

- intentional time together—time to laugh, cry, eat mandarin oranges, and share hilarious life stories
- countless meals and visits with her lifelong friends
- Kay's celebrating the little things—like a University of Georgia tennis team victory or a Bojangles blueberry biscuit
- seeing her, even after months of intense treatments, walk proudly down the aisle at a family wedding
- Kay's describing in detail the hospital bedside visit from Jesus, the night before brain surgery. (This was the most priceless story she ever shared with me.)

- precious time for those who loved Kay to tell her what she meant to us

Kay (known by some as KK) was incredibly clear about what she wanted her celebration service to look like. "Everybody needs to wear bright colors, and celebrate." And that's exactly what we did.

She would have been delighted to see her happy place, the Athens Community Theater, filled to capacity with hundreds of people who had come to celebrate her one wild and precious life. The vintage venue looked like a rainbow had exploded with all the bright colors. Each guest was given a purple WWKKD bracelet, reminding us to ask, "What would KK do?" She would smile and thank all of us for coming. Then she'd tell us to not make a big fuss over her...but to go out and do something fun.

It was the honor of a lifetime to speak that day and to share some of our most memorable shenanigans, especially her sacred bedside visit from Jesus story.

How about You?

If you're in a chapter of anticipating the inevitable death of a dear person, the days, months, or even years can be long, hard, and confusing. And even if your loved one's health has been declining for a while, it's hard to balance believing a miracle is still possible with the thought of letting go.

Here are a few ideas that might be helpful as you walk alongside your beloved person.

- Take photos and videos. Record even little moments.

- Save handwritten things.
- Try to get a feel for what kind of memorial service they might want—music, scripture, speakers, or anything else important to them.
- Ask questions. "What was it like when you were a kid?" "Tell me about your first love." "Who is your greatest influence?" Ask whatever might be awesome for generations to come to know about them.
- This might seem super administrative, but ask details about passwords, the location of their will, and end-of-life medical directives.
- Consider one day setting up a legacy account in their honor on Facebook.
- Take care of you. What you're going through is intense, but this time can create wonderful memories with your loved one.

Feel free to use these pages to write anything that comes to mind about your anticipatory grief.

Beth Marshall

Bonus Chapter Two

Quick, Slow, Slow—Anger Management 101

T he kids are playing, laughing, and being loud, and from out of nowhere, you lose your patience and raise your voice at them. A friend or coworker asks the same question they ask every day, but today you fire back with a snarky remark. The driver in front of you takes that extra split second when the light turns green, and you lay on the horn, wondering how they can be so annoying.

Maybe you find yourself reacting quickly, in a sarcastic tone that doesn't line up with your characteristically cheerful disposition.

What's Up?

When you've been sideswiped by sorrow, sometimes it's not the thing that makes you snap. It's the thing beneath the thing.

> *It's the grief talking—coming out sideways, when it has nowhere to go.*

It's the grief talking—coming out sideways, when it has nowhere to go.

Sleepless nights, combined with chaotic days and a restless heart, can create the perfect storm for anger to launch an ambush on the people we love most.

So What's the Solution?

I wish there was a ten-step anger management plan for adversity and grief-related anger, but, until then, I'm thankful we serve a forgiving and loving God who understands.

He's there on the good days and on the days your kindness, compassion, and compelling-sense-of-humor filter are broken.

> *He's there on the good days and on the days your kindness, compassion, and compelling-sense-of-humor filter are broken.*

The Dance

Are you a dancer? I wasn't. Then I married into a family of hard-core dancers. My husband, Paul's people never needed an excuse to break out into a dance party. Anytime was the right time for a quick cha-cha-cha or rumba. In fact, the classic quick, quick, slow rhythm of the rumba is the first dance Paul attempted to teach me.

Whenever I catch myself with a sarcastic, not-exactly-loving retort on the tip of my tongue, the compelling words from James 1:19 rush to the forefront of my mind.

- **quick** to listen

- **slow** to speak
- **slow** to become angry

Ouch.

Instead of the *quick, quick, slow* cadence of the rumba, I try to mentally flip the script to *quick, slow, slow.* The new rhythm might not win a dance contest, but it will inevitably remind me to

- take a breath
- take a second to run the snarky thought through the quick, slow, slow (quick to listen, slow to speak, slow to become angry) grid
- exhale slowly
- take another breath—and then, hopefully I will have forgotten the snappy remark altogether

I wish I could say this newly revised quick, slow, slow filter picks up every stray or hurtful comment before it is launched—it doesn't, but it's a start. Lord, help me.

How about You?

If grief-related anger has crept into your life, you are not alone. I invite you to use these pages to write any ideas you have for dealing with anger. The struggle is real.

Thanks, I needed that.

_____

_____

_____

_____

_____

_____

_____

_____

_____

_____

_____

_____

_____

_____

_____

_____

_____

_____

Beth Marshall

_____

_____

_____

_____

_____

_____

_____

_____

_____

_____

_____

_____

_____

_____

_____

_____

_____

_____

_____

_____

_____

_____

_____

_____

_____

_____

_____

_____

_____

_____

_____

_____

_____

_____

_____

_____

Bonus Chapter Three

When Suicide Hits Close to Home

According to the Centers for Disease Control and Prevention, in the United States, one person dies by suicide every eleven minutes. The grim 2020 statistics go on to reveal that suicide is one of the top nine leading causes of death in the US for all ages and the second leading cause of death for youth and young adults between the ages of 10–14 and 25–34.

You never think your family will become a part of such heartbreaking statistics.

The collateral damage caused by suicide is immeasurable and can last for generations.

My Family's Story

I wish I could have known my Uncle Bob better. Everybody loved him. Sadly, though, I was a little girl at the time of his death. According to his mother, his sisters,

> *The collateral damage caused by suicide is immeasurable and can last for generations*

and his now-adult kids, he was incredibly social, thoughtful to bring the family gifts from business trips, and brilliant. Bob graduated at the top of his class and was voted Most Likely to Succeed. He loved to host parties, had lots of friends, a terrific job, a lovely home, a beautiful thirty-two-year-old wife, and four kids, ages seven, six, four, and two, who adored him.

A few months after his family's move to their dream home, during a sailing vacation with friends, something in Uncle Bob's mind seemed to snap. Those closest to him described what happened as a "nervous breakdown." I'm not sure what his exact diagnosis would be called now, but whatever happened resulted in a long hospitalization in a psychiatric facility. Some of his kids remember visiting him with their mom on Sundays.

Bob was released from the hospital with what my Aunt Linda describes as experimental medication. No one is sure exactly what was prescribed, but antidepressant meds were pretty new to the market in the 1960s. His kids describe him as being really different after the hospital stay. He would spend most of his time alone in the basement, assembling model trains, airplanes, and battleships.

My cousin David remembers the day his dad died. "Dad left for good, in an ambulance but with no siren. Mom never told us how he died. We saw the police cars and the ambulance, but we never saw our father again."

At the time of his death, topics like depression, hopelessness, and anxiety were rarely discussed. With a physical illness, broken bone, or disease, it was perfectly acceptable to go to the doctor, get a diagnosis, maybe a prescription, and tell all your friends about it.

Sadly, conversations around mental health challenges were not so common. People were expected to be okay, or at least pretend they were.

> *Sadly, conversations around mental health challenges were not so common. People were expected to be okay, or at least pretend they were.*

What Now?

We may never fully understand the circumstances that lead up to a heart-shattering death by suicide. My prayer is that counseling and treatment for anxiety and depression, as well as honest and open discussions around mental health, become as easily accessible as any other kind of medical treatment.

If suicide loss is part of your family's story, you understand that the deep sorrow for those left behind is like no other. In the devastating aftermath, survivors often feel overwhelmed with guilt, shame, intense sorrow, anger, and countless unanswered questions.

Could I have done something to prevent what happened?
Were there signs we should have seen?
Am I somehow to blame?

As I look back, there are a few things I wish someone had told our family:

- You may never understand why your loved one died the way they did, but it is not your fault.
- Don't go through this by yourself. Talk to someone—a pastor, grief counselor, or a support group can help you feel less alone.

- Over time you'll hopefully be able to focus on the goodness of their life, instead of exclusively on the circumstances around their death. Journaling and saving photos can help stir up memories of happier times.

Here are a few things my cousins shared with me—

Cousin Robert (seven at the time) remembers his dad being a positive influence for him—and that he probably inherited his sense of responsibility from his father. Robert also remembers feeling anger for a lot of years.

Robert currently serves as a Stephen Minister in his church—providing one-on-one, Christ-centered care for people in the congregation and community experiencing life difficulties.

Cousin David (six at the time)—"If I could say something to my father, it would probably just be this: I forgive you and I'm sorry you were not here to share our joys and to help us deal with our sorrows.

"Probably my biggest regret/struggle associated with growing up without a father is that I was never trained to be one. I had to educate myself by observing neighbors, coaches, teachers, and relatives, including Uncle John."

Cousin Susan (four at the time) realized after years of therapy that she "had to go through the sadness to get to the other side." She couldn't go around it. I asked Susan if there was anything she'd want to say to her dad if she could. "I'd want to say 'I love you, and I understand. I hope you're out of your pain. I miss you. I would have loved to have had a dad.'"

She added, "I hope our kids understand it's okay to ask for help."

Cousin Becky (two at the time) doesn't remember much about her dad. She didn't hear how he died 'til she was sixteen. It was the shock of her life. Becky clings dearly to the photos she has of him.

"It's easy to lose hope when you're feeling overwhelmed. It's hard to keep trusting, hoping, or believing when you feel like you're being crushed by the pressures of life. The enemy of our souls loves to take advantage of those times of weakness, confusion, disappointment, or grief. He wants you to believe it's all over, there's no light at the end of the tunnel, and that you should give up. I'm here to remind you that this is not the end. This thing will not take you out. Your God loves you, sees you, hears you, and is with you. He has not left you. He has not forsaken you. You can trust God even when you can't trace Him. Jesus is trustworthy." Thank you, gospel teacher and international speaker Christine Caine.

Finding Help

Depression, anxiety, a family history of suicide, or a traumatic life event can increase intense feelings of helplessness. The pain you feel is real, but suicide is never the solution.

If you or someone you know is considering harming themselves, **seek immediate treatment.** Call 911, go to the local emergency room, or call a local crisis response team. The time to act is now.

You can also seek 24/7 support through National Suicide Prevention Lifeline by dialing 988.

Bonus Chapter Four

Uncrushed Faith

Wherever you are on your faith journey—maybe you're still kicking the tires to see if faith is even something you want to know more about—it's okay. I get it. For twenty-seven years, that was one hundred percent me. And even since the morning I desperately prayed, "Jesus, if You're real, I need You. I can't do this by myself anymore," *I still have a lot of questions.*

What I'm slowly learning, though, is that what *I do know* to be true about the Lord is more important than all the things I don't fully understand yet. What I do know is that...

- He loves me and He loves YOU more than words can say. He loved us enough to give His life for us.
- He sees us—when we're awake, when we're asleep, when we laugh, when we can't stop crying, when we're angry, when our heart is peaceful, when we feel all alone in our pain, He sees us.

When Jesus' dear friend Lazurus died, the fact that "Jesus wept" (John 11:35, NIV) helps us know that He was no stranger to grief, loss, and pain.

Confession of a "Cool-on-a-Coffee-Cup" Scripture Memorizer

Before losing several of my closest and favorite humans, I had committed a few well-known passages of scripture to memory—but had never needed them as desperately as I do now. The memorized words that had once been "cool-on-a-coffee-cup," familiar sayings to me were now sinking deeply into my heart, as I began to face the tumultuous waters of deep loss.

For the first time ever, I realized what a precious lifeline God's word can be and how He really can be trusted.

Here are a few verses that continue to speak sweet comfort to my soul, even when heartache and loss come. Please indulge me as I share a bit of personal commentary.

"The Lord gives his people strength. The Lord blesses them with peace." Psalm 29:11, NLT

Yep. He really will bless us with His strength and peace. I'm actually experiencing both right this minute, as I write these words for you.

"So we fix our eyes not on what is seen, but on what is unseen, since what is seen is temporary, but what is unseen is eternal." 2 Corinthians 4:18, NIV

It's always been pretty hard for me to trust things I couldn't actually see and touch, but I'm pretty sure the hard-to-understand things in this world will make more sense when we see the Lord face-to-face.

"The Lord is close to the brokenhearted and saves those who are crushed in spirit." Psalm 34:18, NIV

These profound words have been pure oxygen for me

through times of deep loss and heartbreak. If there's one thing I hope you take from these pages, it's that no pain is beyond the Lord's ability to touch and comfort.

"Blessed are those who mourn, for they will be comforted." Matthew 5:4, NIV

I'm living proof of this one.

"May the God of hope fill you with all joy and peace as you trust in him, so that you may overflow with hope by the power of the Holy Spirit." Romans 15:13, NIV

Amen, let it be so, Lord!

Father, for the person reading these words today who's feeling hopeless, alone, or crushed, please hold this dear son or daughter close to Your loving heart. Bring Your indescribable peace and healing, by Your mighty resurrection power. Amen.

Special Thanks

To my family—Paul, Michael, Morgan, Caroline, Nick, Amy, Carter, Grayson, Annie, Jane, and Greta—I love you guys with my whole heart. Thanks for believing in me and cheering me on!

To the *Uncrushed* Prayer Warriors—Dalton Blankenship, Sherry Cooley, Lee McDerment, Deb Morgan, Joanna Neal, Barb Ready, Wanda Staggers, Dorothy Jenkins, Tara-Leigh Cobble, Jeff Henderson, and my sister/cousin Turner Lawton. Every single prayer you prayed for me and for this book mattered. Your unwavering kindness and love mean the world to me.

To Lysa TerKeurst, Meredith Brock, and Coach Nicki Koziarz—Book Proposal Boot Camp was one wild, crazy, intense, challenging, life-changing ride. Thank you!

To Bob Goff and Kimberly Stuart—You and **The Writer's Workshop** gave me the courage to keep writing, connect with an amazing publisher, and get *Uncrushed* out into the world!

To all the wonderful friends and family members whose stories fill the pages of this book— Amy Marshall, Sharie King, Josh Bull, Kelly Rodes, Clayton King, Mandy Smith, Nicki Koziarz, Whitney and Nick Kirby, Aimee Myers,

Dorothy Jenkins, Davey Blackburn, Robert Montgomery, David Montgomery, Susan Montgomery Morrison, and Becky Montgomery Tucker—Your loved one's legacy is still shining brightly through you. Thank you for sharing a bit of their extraordinary story in Uncrushed.

To Victoria Duerstock, Hope Bolinger, Nikki Wright, and End Game Press—what an honor it is to be part of your team!!

Notes and References

Chapter Two

1. Sharie King (@SharieKing99), "I lost my dad today...", Instagram photo, January 5, 2021, https://www.instagram.com/p/CJsKQElFsig/?igshid=YmMyMTA2M2Y=.

Chapter Three

1. Miles Adcox, "Dreaming in the Time of Coronavirus," April 2020, in *Dream Big Podcast with Bob Goff and Friends,* produced by Tatave Abeshyan and Haley King, podcast, MP3 audio, https://podcasts.apple.com/us/podcast/miles-adcox-dreaming-in-the-time-of-coronavirus/.

Chapter Four

1. Bob Goff, "Comparison Is a Punk" (lecture, *Writer's Workshop,* April 2021).

Chapter Five

1. "Motherless Daughters Australia: Home," Motherless Daughters Australia, https://www.motherlessdaughters.com.au/.

2. "The Compassionate Friends: Home," The Compassionate Friends, https://www.compassionatefriends.org/.

Chapter Seven

1. Anne Lamott, "Anne Lamott: Quotes," Goodreads, https://www.goodreads.com/author/quotes/7113.Anne_Lamott.

2. Tara-Leigh Cobble, "…a theological disaster…" Facebook comment to Beth Marshall, 2021, http://www.facebook.com/lizgmarshall/, quote used by permission from Tara-Leigh Cobble, December 15, 2022.

3. Rick Warren, "How to Get Through What You're Going Through" (lecture, Saddleback Church) https://saddleback.com/watch/how-to-get-through-what-youre-going-through/.

Chapter Ten

1. @GriefKid, "I didn't call because," Instagram stories, 2021, https://www.instagram.com/griefkid/.

Chapter Eleven

1. Joshua Bull, *Time with God,* used by permission, April 21, 2021.

Chapter Twelve

1. Fran Meyer-Drasutis, "Grief Is Like Swimming in Peanut Butter" (lecture, American Widow Project Getaway, 2015).

2. Dr. Tony Evans (@drtonyevans), "Sometimes God lets you hit rock bottom…" Twitter, August 7, 2020, https://twitter.com/drtonyevans/status/12917494748500815874?lang=en.

Chapter Thirteen

1. Lysa TerKeurst, *Forgiving What You Can't Forget: Discover How to Move On, Make Peace with Painful Memories, and Create a Life That's Beautiful Again,* (Nashville, TN, Thomas Nelson, 2020).

2. Lysa TerKeurst, "Lysa TerKeurst:Quotes," Goodreads, https://www.goodreads.com/work/

quotes/78429062-forgiving-what-you-can-t-forget-discover-how-to-move-on-make-peace-wit

Chapter Fourteen

1. "Grief Quotes," Normalize Grief | @GlitterAndGrief, https://www.normalizegrief.com/grief-quotes/.

2. Pastor Rick Warren (@PastorRickWarren), "Grief comes in waves," Instagram stories, https://www.instagram.com/pastorrickwarren/.

3. Tamsin Millard, "How can I process my complicated grief? With Dr. Chloe," April 1, 2021, in *Not So Linear Podcast*, podcast, MP3 audio, https.//podcasts.apple.com/us/podcast/not-so-linear/id1553150490?i=1000515470585.

Chapter Fifteen

1. Nora McInerny, "We Don't 'Move On' from Grief. We Move Forward with It" (lecture, *TED Talk*) https://www.ted.com/talks/nora_mcinerny_we_don_t_move_on_from_grief_we_move_forward_with_it.

2. Lysa TerKeurst, group text, Fall 2021.

Chapter Sixteen

1. Bob Goff (lecture, *Writer's Workshop*, April 2021).

Chapter Seventeen

1. Lysa TerKeurst @LysaTerkeurst, "I can sit with Jesus, Instagram stories, 2022., https://www.instarram.com/lysaterkeurst/.

Chapter Eighteen

1. Jacinta Wilson (JacintaWilson) Facebook post, December 20, 2021, *Good Mourning Grief Community,* https://

wwwfacebook.com/groups/goodmourningcommunity/
permalink/1494550954278687/.

Chapter Twenty-Two

1. Zac Smith, "Despite Cancer, God Is Still God, and God Is Still Good," NewSpring Church Stories, NewSpring.cc, May 4, 2010, https://newspring.cc/stories/zacsmith.

Chapter Twenty-Four

1. Sharie King (@SharieKing99), "Father's Day is usually...," Instagram, June 10, 2021, https://www.instagram.com/p/CP9drUmtK1o/?igshid=YmMyMTA2M2Y=.

2. Whitney Kirby, https://www.facebook.com/whitneyspaughkirby. May 12, 2021.

Chapter Twenty-Five

1. Lysa TerKeurst (@LysaTerKeurst), "If you have a friend going," Instagram stories, Fall 2021, https://www.instagram.com/lysaterkeurst.

2. Dr. Alan Wolfelt (lecture, Hope for the Holidays Conference, November 2014) https://www.centerforloss.com/.

Chapter Twenty-Six

1. Alex Mammadyarov (@AlexMammadyarov), "There is a gentle ease...," Instagram post, July 4, 2021, https://www.instagram.com/p/CSaDmgWFT1k/?igshid=YmMyMTA2M2Y=.

2. Tamsin Millard (@TamsinMillard), "Grief can be lonely" and "When you find your community," Instagram post, November 14, 2021, https://www.instagram.com/reel/CWP3W-3lHaCA3U BYEcmpVvZfUJL9FEqxNFnLfg0/?igshid=YmMyMTA2M2Y=.

3. Beth Marshall and Anna Villanueva, Wanda Weldon, and Anna

Smith, Facebook, https://www.facebook.com/lizgmarshall, link
no longer available.

Chapter Twenty-Eight

1. Megan Margery, "Self-Care Isn't Just Drinking Water," The
   Minds Journal, March 13, 2019, https://themindsjournal.com/
   self-care-isnt-just-drinking-water/.

2. Alex Mammadyarov (@Alex Mammadyarov), "Cry about it,"
   Instagram post, June 24, 2021.

Chapter Thirty

1. "American Widow Project: Home," American Widow Project,
   https://americanwidowproject.org/.

2. Dr. Melanie Riddle, Sherri Bear, and Pattie Riddle, "I always
   embrace the memories," Facebook, December 20, 2021, https://
   www.facebook.com/lizgmarshall.

Chapter Thirty-One

1. Chrystal Evans Hurst (@ChrystalHurst), "It's been a year since,"
   Instagram post, January 6, 2021, https://www.instagram.com/p/
   CJteBjZAiW2/?igshid=YmMyMTA2M2Y=.

Chapter Thirty-Two

1. HopeMommies.org.

Chapter Thirty-Four

1. Anna Meyer-Shine, "How Making a 'Reverse Bucket
   List' Can Make You Happier," Fast Company, November
   20, 2017, https://www.fastcompany.com/40497651/
   how-making-a-reverse-bucket-list-can-make-you-happier.

2. Nicki Koziarz, "Gratitude When Things Don't Go Our
   Way," November 12, 2020, in Lessons from the Farm Podcast,

podcast, MP3 audio, https://nickikoziarz.com/2020/11/episode-55gratitude-when-things-dont-go-our-way/.

3.   Bob Goff (lecture, *Writer's Workshop*, April 2021).

Chapter Thirty-Five

1.   Tamsin Millard, "How can I process my complicated grief? With Dr. Chloe," April 1, 2021, in *Not So Linear Podcast*, podcast, MP3 audio, https://open.spotify.com/episode/2sLjk2O5jzdNWELbbDgHbp.

2.   Donald Miller, "…the most beautiful, selfless people…" Facebook, March 18, 2021, https://www.facebook.com/donaldmillerwords.

Chapter Thirty-Six

1.   LuAnn Whyte Scruggs, Founder of *Blooming Again* grief recovery Facebook group, https://www.facebook.com/groups/118709556806730.

2.   Kristy Furlow, "Cloth & Clay: Home," Cloth & Clay, https://clothandclay.org/.

3.   Thrive (@Thrive), "Surround yourself with people," Instagram story, 2021, https://www.instagram.com/thrive.

Chapter Thirty-Seven

1.   Davey Blackburn, Nothing Is Wasted Ministries, https://www.nothingiswasted.com/, homepage.

2.   Ibid.

3.   Dr. Gloria Horsley and Dr. Heidi Horsley, Co-founders of Open to Hope Foundation, https://www.opentohope.com/.

Chapter Thirty-Nine

1. The Grief Toolbox (@The-grief-toolbox), "There's a fear I have," Instagram story, 2021, https://thegrieftoolbox.com/.

2. Geneva Livingstone (@Death-Etiquette, Instagram stories, April 2021, https://www.instagram.com/death_etiquette/.

Bonus Chapter One

1. Amy Marshall, "Rockin' with My Grandma," Poem.

Bonus Chapter Three

1. "Facts about Suicide," Centers for Disease Control and Prevention, May 24, 2022, https://www.cdc.gov/suicide/facts/index.html.

2. Christine Caine (@ChristineCaine), "It's easy to lose hope," Facebook, April 5, 2022 https://www.facebook.com/ChristineCaine.

About the Author

B eth Marshall is wife to her best boyfriend/husband, Paul, mom to three grown kids, and "Lali" to five next-generation superheroes (lovable grandpeople).

After the shocking death of her mom, "Beazy," Beth searched desperately for a resource that might touch the deep pain she was experiencing. Nothing on the market seemed to help. One morning, she felt a nudge from the Lord to start writing about her mom in her journal. As she recorded sweet, sentimental, and hilarious memories of life with Beazy, she realized her one-of-a-kind mom would not be forgotten.

Journaling through grief was the catalyst for Beth to start writing books and speaking to help others who had loved and lost a dear person in their lives.

After a twenty-five year career as a flight attendant with Delta Air Lines, Beth served as Care Ministry Coordinator for NewSpring Church. She's the author of *Grief Survivor—28 steps toward hope and healing* and *A Time to Heal: A Grief*

Journal, and she has written two study plans for the YouVersion app: *Grief Survivor* and *More Than You Can Handle.*

Beth and Paul live in North Carolina and love spending time with their grown kids, kids-in-law, and grandkids in the mountains and at the South Carolina coast.